Global Perspectives

Listening & Speaking Book 2

by

Noriko Nakanishi

Nicholas Musty

Shoko Otake

Tam Shuet Ying

Yuki Ebihara

Keiji Fujimura

JN062937

音声ファイルのダウンロード／ストリーミング

CD マーク表示がある箇所は、音声を弊社 HP より無料でダウンロード／ストリーミングすることができます。下記 URL の書籍詳細ページに音声ダウンロードアイコンがございますのでそちらから自習用音声としてご活用ください。

http://seibido.co.jp/ad660

Global Perspectives
Listening & Speaking Book 2

はしがき

　自動翻訳機能や自動音声認識技術の発達のおかげで、自分で英文を考えたり聞き取ったりしなくても、趣味の旅行程度の簡単な英語会話には不自由しない時代になりました。しかし、単に目的地までの道順を尋ねたりレストランで食事を注文したりするだけでなく、会話の相手と交流を深めたり意見を交わしたりするには、自分の耳でニュアンスを聞き取って論点を整理し、相手の文化や考え方の背景を尊重しながら自分の考えを自分の言葉で伝えなければ、本当の意味でのコミュニケーションは成り立ちません。

　さらに、日本国内にいても日本語を母語としない人々と接する機会は多くあります。世界的な感染症拡大の影響により、自宅に居ながらもオンラインで海外の人々とコミュニケーションをとる環境が整いつつあります。これまでのビジネスシーンでは海外出張とは無縁だった人も、各国の人々と英語で会話をすることが日常となる将来は近いでしょう。世界の人口比や経済活動の状況を考えると、会話の相手は、英語のネイティブ・スピーカーとは限りません。世界各地域の言語的特徴の影響を受けた多様な英語を尊重する「世界諸英語（World Englishes）」という捉え方が必要とされます。英語の多様性だけでなく、文化や習慣・価値観の多様性にも配慮しながら、自分の考えを分かりやすく伝えるコミュニケーション力が、今後の社会では一層求められます。

　本書のねらいは、学習者が大学入学までに培ってきた以下の「三つの柱（文部科学省、2018 年 3 月公示）」を引き継ぎ、さらに発展させることです。

　　（1）何を理解しているか、何ができるか（知識・技能）
　　（2）理解していること・できることをどう使うか（思考力・判断力・表現力）
　　（3）どのように社会・世界と関わり、よりよい人生を送るか（学びに向かう力・人間性）

　本書の Book 1 では大学生が日常的に経験する「大学生活」「心と体の健康」のようなトピック、Book 2 では「学術研究」「科学とは」のような、大学生にふさわしい学際的なトピックを扱います。Unit ごとのトピックに関連する会話やモノローグを聞いて英語リスニング力を養うだけでなく、情報を整理し、多様な角度から検討した上で、論理的・客観的に自分の意見を述べるための批判的思考力をつけることを目的としています。異なった言語背景・文化背景を持つ話者間のやり取りや、賛否が分かれることがらについてのモノローグ音声を元に、自分の意見を整理して英語で述べるための発表アウトラインの作成へとつなげます。本書を通して、学習者が英語のリスニング力やスピーキング力を伸ばすだけでなく、思考力・判断力・表現力や積極性・人間性を養うきっかけとなることを願っています。

　最後に、本書の出版にあたり、趣旨をご理解くださり、きめ細やかなアドバイスでサポートくださった（株）成美堂編集部の中澤ひろ子氏に、心から感謝を申し上げます。

2022 年 10 月
筆者一同

本書の構成 / 使い方

❶ Warm-up

各ユニットに関連したトピックについて4つの選択肢の中から自分の知識や考えに近いものを選び、ウォーミングアップをしましょう。時間に余裕があれば、なぜその選択肢を選んだか説明し、クラスメイトと意見交換しましょう。

❷ Words in focus

各ユニットに関連した用語を予め確認しましょう。単に英単語を和訳するのではなく、用語をネット検索して、トピックと関連する背景知識を身につけておきましょう。

❸ Dialogue

日本の大学生ケンとマリが、世界諸英語の話者と会話します。会話の内容だけでなく、地域特有の語彙・綴り・発音にも注目しましょう。Unit 1-5 はアメリカ・イギリス・オセアニア出身者、Unit 6 以降では、シンガポール・インド・ロシア・ラテンアメリカ・中国・エジプト・アフリカ出身者が登場します。

内容理解問題は5つの <Scene> に分かれています。<Scene> 1, 2 では日常の会話で使えそうなフレーズが穴埋め問題になっています。<Scene> 3-5 は、台本がテキストに掲載されていません。先に問題に目を通してから必要な情報を聞き取る練習をしましょう。

❹ Viewpoints

Dialogue をもう一度聞きながら内容語を書き取り、<Scene> 1-5 の要点をまとめましょう。

❺ Pronunciation

Dialogue の中で、英語の音声的な特徴が表れている部分をもう一度聞き、聞き取りや発音のコツをつかみましょう。

❻ Monologue

大学での講義やスピーチ・アナウンス・トークショーのような1人の話者によるトークを聞きながら、必要に応じて図表などを参考に、内容を理解しましょう。トークを聞く前に、やや難易度が高い語の意味と発音を確認しておきましょう。

内容理解問題の後で、スクリプトを見ながらもう一度トークを聞き、やや難易度が高い語を書き取りましょう。前ページで確認した語とは語形が異なるものがあるため、文法知識も必要です。

❼ Speaking outline

ユニットに関連したトピックで口頭発表をするためのアウトラインをまとめましょう。アウトラインは、基本的に「Introduction（導入）」と「Conclusion（結論）」の間に「Body（本論）」を挟み込む構成になっています。以下は、各ユニットで紹介されるアウトライン作成のコツです。

Unit	コツ	Unit	コツ
1	Main idea and details (1)	7	Sequencing
2	Dealing with unknown words	8	Comparison and contrast
3	Cause and effect	9	Main idea and details (2)
4	Understanding timelines	10	Inference (1)
5	Similarities and differences	11	Inference (2)
6	Categorization	12	Paraphrasing

CONTENTS

EnglishCentralのご案内

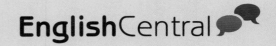

　本テキスト各ユニットの「Dialogue」のconversationと「Monologue」で学習する音声は、オンライン学習システム「EnglishCentral」で学習することができます。

　EnglishCentralでは動画の視聴や単語のディクテーションのほか、動画のセリフを音読し録音すると、コンピュータが発音を判定します。PCのwebだけでなく、スマートフォン、タブレットではアプリでも学習できます。リスニング、スピーキング、語彙力向上のため、ぜひ活用してください。

　EnglishCentralの利用にはアカウントとアクセスコードの登録が必要です。登録方法については下記ページにアクセスしてください。

（画像はすべてサンプルで、実際の教材とは異なります）

https://www.seibido.co.jp/englishcentral/pdf/ectextregister.pdf

見る

本文内でわからなかった単語は1クリックでその場で意味を確認

スロー再生

日英字幕（ON/OFF可）

学ぶ

音声を聴いて空欄の単語をタイピング。ゲーム感覚で楽しく単語を覚える

話す

動画のセリフを音読し録音、コンピュータが発音を判定。

日本人向けに専門開発された音声認識によってスピーキング力を%で判定

ネイティブと自分が録音した発音を聞き比べ練習に生かすことができます

苦手な発音記号を的確に判断し、単語を緑、黄、赤の3色で表示

Academic Research

学術的な研究について考えよう

Warm-up: *Share your ideas.*

How much do you know about in-text citations?

a. I do not know anything about it.

b. I have heard a little about it.

c. I have studied it.

d. I can write essays following the rule.

I chose answer _____, because...
....
....
....

Words in focus: *Search the internet for words and phrases.* 1-02

❏ APA style manual

❏ argument

❏ author

❏ edited paper

❏ in-text citation

❏ plagiarism

❏ publication date

❏ reference

❏ source

❏ Writing 101

Dialogue

■ *Why do we need correct in-text citations?*

1. Listen to each phrase, and guess what the speaker implies. 🄲🄳 1-03

1. (   )
2. (   )
3. (   )

> (A) We will focus on this part together.
>
> (B) You must have worked hard.
>
> (C) People's views may differ depending on the environment in which they grew up.

2. Listen to the conversation and fill in the blanks. 🄲🄳 1-04,05

Ken is talking with Ms. Smith, a professor from the United States.

<Scene 1>

Ken: Professor, how was my psychology paper?

Prof. Smith: Hello, Ken. I hate to tell you this, but you're going to have to rewrite some parts.

Ken: Oh, no! What did I do wrong?

Prof. Smith: Ken, (1) _____,
but there are a few things I'd like you to fix. Do you have your APA style manual with you today?

Ken: Yes, I do. Here it is. I'm glad that I brought this with me.

Prof. Smith: Great. Let's go over your paper together then.

The Müller-Lyer Illusion

<Scene 2>

Ken: Here's my list of references.

Prof. Smith: (2) _____ Great, they're articles about the Müller-Lyer illusion.

Ken: Yes, I was arguing in my paper that (3) _____
_____ that only works in modern, industrialized societies.

Prof. Smith: Yes, that argument was good. However, take a look at your in-text citations.

Ken: So, the in-text citations are supposed to be after each sentence, right?

Prof. Smith: Yes. The manual says you also need the author's last name and the year of publication.

3. Listen to the conversation again and choose the best answer to each question. (repeat)  1-04, 05

<Scene 1> Why did Professor Smith mention the APA manual?

(A) She wants Ken to buy it soon.

(B) She needs Ken to fix the manual.

(C) She wishes to use it to go over Ken's paper.

(D) She hates using the manual.

<Scene 2> According to Professor Smith, what do you need in an in-text citation?

(A) The author's first name and the year of publication.

(B) The author's last name and the year of publication.

(C) A paragraph explaining visual illusions.

(D) A paragraph describing APA citations.

4. Listen to scenes 3 to 5, and choose the best answer to each question. 1-06, 07, 08

<Scene 3> What was wrong with Ken's paper?

(A) He copied his friend's paper.

(B) His argument was not strong enough.

(C) The author's name was missing in his citation.

(D) The year of publication was missing in his citation.

<Scene 4> What did Ken find out about scientific facts?

(A) Scientific exceptions may change over time.

(B) All scientific facts are in textbooks.

(C) Visual illusions don't work for him.

(D) Scientific facts do not have exceptions.

<Scene 5> Which of the following is Ken NOT likely to do?

(A) Add the year of publication to his citation.

(B) Hand-write his whole paper.

(C) Look for more recent papers to support his argument.

(D) Submit the edited paper to Professor Smith.

▍Viewpoints

(repeat) 🎵 CD 1-04, 05, 06, 07, 08

ケンがなぜレポートを修正しなければならないかが表れているフレーズをもう一度聞き、書き取りましょう。

<Scene 1> 修正が必要	**Prof. Smith:** I hate to tell you this, but you're _g_____ to _h_____ to _r_____ _s____ _p_____.
<Scene 2> 文中引用に 記載すること	**Ken:** So, the in-text citations are supposed to be _a_____ _e_____ _s_____, right? **Prof. Smith:** The manual says you also need the _a_____ _l____ _n_____ and the _y____ of _p_____.
<Scene 3> 出版年の 重要性	**Ken:** Oops! I _f_____ to _in_____ the _y____. **Prof. Smith:** _Ps_____ is a type of _sc_____, and the _p_____ _d___ _m_____ a lot.
<Scene 4> 真実は時とともに変わる	**Prof. Smith:** But when you learn things at _c_____, _sc_____ _f_____ can have _e_____. **Ken:** So _f_____ and _e_____ in _____ might be _d_____ from ones in _____.
<Scene 5> 著者名と 出版年	**Prof. Smith:** To show how _sc_____ _i_____ _ch_____, you need to show the reader which year each finding was _p_____. **Ken:** So this article should be _c_____ as (Pedersen & Wheeler, 1983), right?

▍World Englishes （世界の英語）

同じ英語でも話者の出身地によって、語彙・綴り・発音などが異なることがあります。

【語彙】この Unit でスミス先生はケンが大学に入学するまでの教育機関を "high school" と表現していますが、"secondary school" と呼ぶ地域も世界にはあります。

【綴り】Unit 4 でお母さんのことをジャックの発言では "mum"、マリの発言では "mom" と綴りました。これは、ジャックの出身地アイルランドではイギリス式綴り、マリの出身地日本ではアメリカ式綴りが使われることが多いためです。

【発音】英和辞書にはたいていアメリカ発音とイギリス発音が掲載されていますが、英語は世界の多くの地域で話されているため、辞書に掲載されている発音しか認められないわけではありません。世界の誰とでも会話できるよう、多様な英語を聞き取れるよう練習しましょう。

Monologue

■ *Welcome to Writing 101.*

1. Choose the phrase that is related to each word, and practice reading it out loud. 🎧 1-09

1. address	( )	(a) an important subject or problem
2. assume	( )	(b) an official group with power
3. authority	( )	(c) correctly
4. edit	( )	(d) needed
5. expel	( )	(e) reasonable and acceptable
6. issue	( )	(f) to make a change or correction
7. legitimate	( )	(g) to deal with a problem
8. properly	( )	(h) to make someone leave a school
9. required	( )	(i) to think that something is likely to be true
10. source	( )	(j) someone or something that supplies information

2. Listen to the monologue and choose the best answer to each question. 🎧 1-10

1. What is the main purpose of this lesson?

   (A) To introduce the teacher in this class.

   (B) To teach different skills for writing.

   (C) To emphasize the consequences of plagiarism.

   (D) To show how to use Wikipedia.

2. Look at the notice. What does an "F" mean in this context?

   (A) The name of a course.

   (B) The rank of an award.

   (C) The name of a website.

   (D) The grade of a course.

3. What is one of the reasons that Wikipedia is not recommended?

   (A) Anybody can change the contents.

   (B) It is edited by experts.

   (C) The information is accurate.

   (D) It has the latest information.

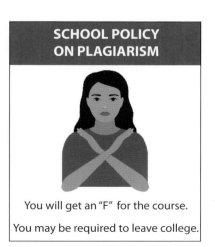

SCHOOL POLICY ON PLAGIARISM

You will get an "F" for the course.
You may be required to leave college.

3. Listen again and fill in the blanks with suitable forms of words in the previous page.

You are attending Professor Smith's first lesson in her writing course. (repeat) 1-10

Hello, everyone, welcome to Writing 101. I'm Angela Smith, and I will be your teacher for this semester. In this class, you will learn the different skills (1) _____ to write at the college level, such as planning, researching, organizing ideas, and (2) _____ your work.

During the semester, one of the most important (3) _____ we will (4) _____ is plagiarism. This is the act of taking someone else's ideas or words, and presenting them as your own. How many of you in the room know this word? Hmm, I see, there are many hands up in the air, so I'm (5) _____ that many of you already know that it is wrong to copy from somebody else.

As you may have guessed, plagiarism is not tolerated in this class. I use plagiarism checker websites to check your essays. If I do find that a student did plagiarize, they will fail the class, and I will have to report them to the college (6) _____. It is likely that they will also be expelled from college. One of my best friends from college plagiarized from Wikipedia for her writing class. I think she did it because she had trouble finishing her work on time. Unfortunately, she was (7) _____.

Oh, a question? So the question was, "Can we use Wikipedia if we (8) _____ cite it?" Great question. As a general rule, please don't use it. This is because unlike other websites, Wikipedia articles can be edited by anyone, including people who aren't experts on the topic. We can never be sure that the information is correct, or up to date. During the semester, I'm hoping to also discuss which websites are (9) _____ (10) _____ and which are not.

Speaking outline: *Main idea and details* (1)
 1-11

For academic research, what kind of source do you recommend? What are the advantages and disadvantages of that source?

1) Main idea	Books / Academic journals / Official database / Web pages / Mass media can be an important source for conducting academic research. I will describe an advantage and a disadvantage of this kind of source.
2) Detail 1 Advantage	One of the advantages of _____ is _____. For example, _____.
3) Detail 2 Disadvantage	On the other hand, a disadvantage of _____ is _____. For example, _____.
4) Conclusion	In conclusion, _____.

Social Issues in Japan

日本の社会について考えよう

Warm-up: *Share your ideas.*

Which of the following issues of modern society are you most interested in? Why?

a. Elderly care.

b. Non-regular employment.

c. Population disparity.

d. Universal design.

> *I chose answer _____, because...*
> ....
> ....
> ....

Words in focus: *Search the internet for words and phrases.*

 1-12

❏ elderly parents

❏ job hunting

❏ mid-career recruitment

❏ mock job interview

❏ pension

❏ the bubble burst

❏ the Cabinet Office

❏ the Covid-19 crisis

❏ the employment ice age generation

❏ unemployed

Dialogue

How many people are between jobs?

1. Listen to each phrase, and guess what the speaker implies. 1-13

1. (   )   (A) Describe the group of people for me.

2. (   )   (B) We could have helped them before.

3. (   )   (C) You could wait for a while.

2. Listen to the conversation and fill in the blanks.

Lucas is an international student from the USA. He is talking to Mari.   1-14, 15

<Scene 1>

Lucas: Mari, why are you wearing a dark suit today?

Mari: I had a mock job interview this morning.

Lucas: You already started preparing for job hunting?

Mari: Of course, because I need a job after I graduate.

Lucas: (1) _____

You still have things to do in college.

Mari: No, the earlier you start, the better job you get.

Lucas: So you want to start working right after graduation.

Mari: Yes, in Japan, mid-career recruitment is not as common as in the U.S.

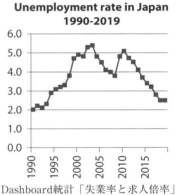

Unemployment rate in Japan 1990-2019

Dashboard統計「失業率と求人倍率」を元に作成

<Scene 2>

Lucas: But I heard that the Japanese government had a program for middle-aged people to get regular jobs.

Mari: Yes, that's for the "employment ice age generation."

Lucas: (2) _____

Mari: It's the age group that finished school after the collapse of the bubble boom.

Lucas: That was around the mid-1990s to the mid-2000s.

Mari: Yes, at that time it was really tough for them to get regular jobs. There are roughly one million people in that generation.

Lucas: (3) _____

Mari: Because the government needs them to pay more tax.

Lucas: I see. If those people get jobs and pay income tax regularly, the government revenue will increase.

Mari: You're right.

8

3. Listen to the conversation again and choose the best answer to each question. (repeat) CD 1-14, 15

\<Scene 1\> Who is getting ready for job hunting?

    (A) Lucas, but not Mari.

    (B) Mari, but not Lucas.

    (C) Both Lucas and Mari.

    (D) Neither Lucas nor Mari.

\<Scene 2\> Who is included in the employment ice age generation?

    (A) Both Lucas and Mari.

    (B) New recruits in Japan.

    (C) Middle-aged people in Japan.

    (D) Workers during the bubble boom.

4. Listen to scenes 3 to 5, and choose the best answer to each question. CD 1-16, 17, 18

\<Scene 3\> Which of the following is NOT included in Mari's explanation about *hikikomori*?

    (A) Many of them are in the employment ice age generation.

    (B) They do not have jobs.

    (C) They are isolated from society.

    (D) They ended the bubble boom.

\<Scene 4\> What is Lucas concerned about?

    (A) How to support his elderly parents.

    (B) At what age people retire from work.

    (C) How the jobless people can earn money.

    (D) At what age people die.

\<Scene 5\> What does "being between jobs" mean?

    (A) working for the government.

    (B) offering trainings.

    (C) having no job at the moment.

    (D) having two jobs at the same time.

Viewpoints

マリとルーカスの会話から日本の就職事情が表れているフレーズをもう一度聞き、書き取りましょう。

\<Scene 1\> 日本での 就職活動	Lucas: Isn't it a bit _t___ _e_____ to _st____? Mari: No, the _e_____ you _st____, the _b_____ _j__ you get. Lucas: So you want to _st____ _w_____ _r___ _a_____ _gr_____. Mari: Yes, in Japan, _m__-c_____ _r_____ is not as _c_____ as in the U.S.
\<Scene 2\> 就職氷河期 世代	Mari: It's the _a___ _gr_____ that _f_____ _s_____ after the _c_____ of the _b_____ _b____. Lucas: That was around the _m___ – ____s to the _m__ – _____s.
\<Scene 3\> 納税できない	Lucas: Even if most of them are _i_____ _w_____, they _st___ _p___ _t_____. Mari: Well, this _g_____ is also _b_____ to _i_____ a large number of _h_____.
\<Scene 4\> ひきこもり	Mari: In most cases, their _e_____ _p_____ are _s_____ them _f_____. Lucas: Then, they will have _n_____ to _d_____ on when their _p_____ _r____ or _p___ _a____.
\<Scene 5\> 政策	Lucas: _Wh___ _k___ of _m_____ does the _g_____ _o_____? Mari: It _o_____ _tr_____ so that they can _st___ _w____ for the _n_____ and _l____ _g_____.

Pronunciation: *Prosody* （韻律）

ルーカスの以下の発話の太字部分の声の強さ・高さ・長さに注意しながら聞いてみましょう。

● You **already** started preparing for job hunting?

すでに就職活動を始めていることに対する驚きを表現している。

● Why do they need support **now**?

なぜ「今になって」必要かを質問している。

音の高さの変化や強さ・高さ・長さなどの音声的な性質（プロソディ）は文字情報だけでは判断できないので、音をよく聞いて話者の意図をくみ取ることが大事です。

Monologue

EC

■ *Anyone can become a hikikomori.*

1. Choose the phrase that is related to each word, and practice reading it out loud. 🎧 1-20

1. confine	( )	**(a)** a feeling of worry or unhappiness
2. conform	( )	**(b)** a time of intense difficulty or danger
3. consecutively	( )	**(c)** an amount of money distributed to elderly people
4. crisis	( )	**(d)** to avoid doing something
5. emerge	( )	**(e)** to be familiar with
6. estimate	( )	**(f)** to behave according to the usual standards
7. guilt	( )	**(g)** to come out
8. pension	( )	**(h)** to guess or calculate the value
9. refrain	( )	**(i)** to keep someone within certain limits of space
10. to be accustomed to	( )	**(j)** without an interruption

2. Listen to the monologue and choose the best answer to each question. 🎧 1-21

1. Which of the following is NOT included in the definition of *hikikomori*?

  (A) Keeping social distance to avoid diseases.

  (B) Not going to work or school.

  (C) Not communicating with people.

  (D) Staying at home for a long period.

2. What is the "80-50 problem"?

  (A) In 2018, 80% of people were unemployed.

  (B) In 2018, 50% of people were *hikikomori*.

  (C) Working-age people depend on their parents.

  (D) Working-age people support their parents.

3. Which of the following is a correct description of the pie chart?

  (A) Many parents are sick.

  (B) About 30% of them are supporting themselves.

  (C) 17% of them work for their wife or husband.

  (D) 6.4% of them work for their brother or sister.

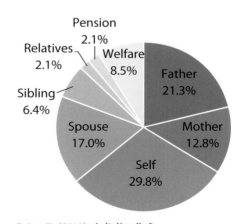

Main source of income in *hikikomori* households

Saito, T（2019）を参考に作成
参考サイト：
https://www.japanpolicyforum.jp/society/pt20190722170048 9609.html

3. Listen again and fill in the blanks with suitable forms of words in the previous page.

You are listening to the news on the *hikikomori* problem in Japan.   (repeat) 🎧 1-21

"Social distance" was an often-heard term at the time of the Covid-19 (1) _____. However, there is another concern about the people who keep too much distance from society.

Hikikomori refers to the lifestyle of people who do not go to work or school. They rarely interact with people other than family members. According to the Japanese health ministry, when people are housebound (2) _____ for six months or longer, they are regarded as *hikikomori*.

The term *hikikomori* was first used in the late 1990s. After the bubble burst, companies (3) _____ from employing new graduates. This hit young people hard. Many of them could not start working full-time. They suffered from feelings of shame and (4) _____. As a result, they found it difficult to (5) _____ to the rules set by society. Thus, those who had withdrawn from society became *hikikomori*.

In 2018, the Cabinet Office conducted a survey. It (6) _____ that 613,000 people aged between 40 and 64 were *hikikomori*. That was when the "80-50 problem" (7) _____ . The problem referred to elderly parents in their 80s and their "children" in their 50s. Those senior citizens had to spend their small incomes and (8) _____ to support their middle-aged children.

After all, the employment situation is not the only cause of the *hikikomori* problem. It can be disasters, accidents or illnesses. There are also people who have left their jobs to look after elderly parents. Some of them have never gone back to work. Bullying is another factor that (9) _____ teenagers in their rooms. After the Covid-19 crisis, people (10) _____ _____ staying home and not interacting with people. Anyone at any age can become a *hikikomori*.

Speaking outline: *Dealing with unknown words*   🎧 1-22

Point out two social phenomena found in Japan. Explain the terms so that people who are not accustomed to Japanese society can understand them.

1) Introduction	Today, I would like to talk about Japanese society. I will focus on _____ and _____.
2) Explanation 1	One of the phenomena in our society is _____. In other words, _____.
3) Explanation 2	_____ is also a typical example to describe our society. That is to say, _____.
4) Conclusion	After all, Japanese society is _____.

Personal Safety

身の回りの安全について考えよう

Warm-up: *Share your ideas.*

When you go abroad, how do you check the safety of the area?

a. Ask my friends.

b. Read somebody's blog.

c. Ask travel agencies.

d. Read the government website.

I chose answer _____, because...

....

....

....

Words in focus: *Search the internet for words and phrases.*

 1-23

❏ belongings

❏ earthquake-prone

❏ emergency

❏ evacuation spot

❏ fake news

❏ legitimate source

❏ misinform

❏ precaution

❏ social media

❏ toxic fumes

Dialogue

■ *London is completely safe?*

1. Listen to each phrase, and guess what the speaker implies.　　🎧 1-24

1. (　　)　　(A) Someone will take it away.

2. (　　)　　(B) What do you want to eat or drink?

3. (　　)　　(C) Nobody will sit here when they see something on the seat.

2. Listen to the conversation and fill in the blanks.　　🎧 1-25, 26

Ken has come to London with Lily, a student in England.

<Scene 1>

Ken: Oh yes! We've finally found Ted's coffee shop! I'm sure this place is famous. It was on Taka's blog.

Lily: That's great to hear. I feel like my feet are going to drop off after all that walking.

Ken: Let's go in. We're lucky, there's a table open right over there. Lily, is that table okay for you?

Lily: Sure. (1) _____
You can save our table while I order for both of us.

Ken: No, you don't have to do that.

<Scene 2>

Ken: (2) _____

Lily: Wait! What are you doing?

Ken: Huh? Did you not like that seat after all?

Lily: Don't just leave your cell phone and other expensive personal stuff lying around!

Ken: Why not?

Lily: (3) _____ If you really want to save a seat, use your hat or scarf.

Ken: Lily, you sound just like my mom. Fine, I'll leave my hat then.

Lily: Great, now let's line up and order. Excuse me, I'd like a cappuccino and carrot cake.

Ken: I want a café mocha and also a piece of apple pie, please.

3. Listen to the conversation again and choose the best answer to each question. (repeat) 🎧 1-25, 26

<Scene 1> What were Ken and Lily doing before this conversation?

  (A) They were meeting Ted.

  (B) They were meeting Taka.

  (C) They were walking around.

  (D) They were ordering food.

<Scene 2> At first, what did Ken want to do to save his seat?

  (A) Leave his bag on the seat.

  (B) Lie on the seat.

  (C) Steal someone's seat.

  (D) Ask his mother.

4. Listen to scenes 3 to 5, and choose the best answer to each question. 🎧 1-27, 28, 29

<Scene 3> Who went to the bathroom?

  (A) Only Ken.

  (B) Only Lily.

  (C) Both Ken and Lily.

  (D) Neither Ken nor Lily.

<Scene 4> Why did Ken feel safe in London?

  (A) Because he had come to London many times.

  (B) Because he read somebody's blog saying that it was safe.

  (C) Because Lily insisted that it was safe.

  (D) Because Lily showed Taka's blog to Ken.

<Scene 5> What is Lily's argument about Ken's attitude?

  (A) He should walk around in daylight.

  (B) He should trust what is written in Taka's blog.

  (C) He should learn basic safety tips.

  (D) He should visit many other dangerous countries.

Viewpoints

ケンとリリーの考え方の違いが表れているフレーズをもう一度聞き、書き取りましょう。

<Scene 1> 観光	**Ken:** We've *f_____ f_____* Ted's *c_____ s_____*! **Lily:** I feel like my *f____* are *g_____* to *d____* off after *a___* that *w_____*.
<Scene 2> 席取り	**Ken:** I can just *s_____* a *s____ u_____* my *b____*. **Lily:** It's *g_____* to be *st_____*.
<Scene 3> 薬物混入	**Ken:** I did *t___* to *m____* it *r_____ f_____* though. **Lily:** *S_____* may *p__ d_____* in them while we are *a_____*.
<Scene 4> ブログ記事の 信頼性	**Lily:** *H____* do you *k_____* Taka is *r_____*? **Ken:** So, it's gotta be *t_____ s_____*.
<Scene 5> 安全性に対する 感覚	**Ken:** But he said "*L_____* is *s_____* for you to *w_____ a_____* in *d_____*". **Lily:** Also, your *i_____* of "*s_____*" can be *d_____* from *h___*.

Pronunciation: *Word and sentence stress*（語強勢・文強勢）

● リリーが注文した cappuccino という語を調べると、たいていの英和辞書では cap·puc·ci·no のように区切られ、この単語が 4 音節に分かれることが示されています。発音記号表記 /kɑ̀ːpətʃíːnou|kæpu-/ の /ɑ̀ː/ や /æ̀/ のように右下がりの記号はその音節に第二強勢、/íː/ のように左下がりの記号はその音節に第一強勢があることを表します。第一強勢、第二強勢の順に強く高く長く発音され、強勢記号がついていない音節には強勢が置かれないので、日本語で「カ・プ・チ・ー・ノ」と言うときのように 5 拍では発音されません。以下の単語の発音をもう一度聞いて、どの音節に強勢が置かれているか確認しましょう。

Lón·don　　Éng·land　　cóf·fee shòp　　fá·mous　　ór·der

● 以下の文の発音をもう一度聞いて、どの音節に強勢が置かれているか確認しましょう。

I'd like a cappuccino and carrot cake.

ひとつの文の中に表れる強勢は文強勢と呼ばれます。基本的に、名詞・動詞・形容詞・副詞のような「内容語」は強勢を置いて発音されますが、冠詞・前置詞・代名詞のような「機能語」には強勢がおかれません。

Monologue

■ *Plan ahead for disasters!*

1. Choose the phrase that is related to each word, and practice reading it out loud. 🔵 1-31

1. accurate	( )	**(a)** correct or exact
2. evacuate	( )	**(b)** often suffering from something
3. fumes	( )	**(c)** poisonous
4. misinform	( )	**(d)** something that people talk about, but may not be true
5. pollute	( )	**(e)** strong and solid
6. precaution	( )	**(f)** strong, unpleasant, and often dangerous gas or smoke
7. prone	( )	**(g)** to give false information
8. rumor	( )	**(h)** to make something dirty or harmful
9. sturdy	( )	**(i)** to move to somewhere safer
10. toxic	( )	**(j)** something that you do to prevent bad things happening in the future

2. Listen to the monologue and choose the best answer to each question. 🔵 1-32

1. Who is this session mainly intended for?

   (A) International students studying in Japan.

   (B) Japanese students on a study abroad program.

   (C) The emergency team dispatched at the time of a disaster.

   (D) Government officials dealing with natural disasters.

2. Which item is NOT mentioned in the session BUT included in the list?

   (A) A passport copy. (C) Flashlight.

   (B) Cash and change. (D) Emergency food and water.

3. According to the talk, what is necessary after an earthquake?

   (A) To lie down on the floor.

   (B) To grab something.

   (C) To get reliable information.

   (D) To spread rumors.

JUIS Disaster Prevention Portal

BEFORE	DURING	AFTER

✓ Practice finding <u>the safest place</u> in your room.
✓ Discuss <u>emergency plans</u> with your family.
✓ Have your <u>emergency bag</u> ready.

- Personal info including allergies, dietary, or medical needs
- A copy of your passport
- Contact phone numbers
- Cash and change, credit card
- Prescription medications
- First aid kit
- Flashlight with extra batteries
- Whistle
- Extra clothing
- Emergency food and water

3. Listen again and fill in the blanks with suitable forms of words in the previous page.

You are attending an orientation session for international students in Japan. (repeat) 🎧 1-32

Hello, students! Welcome to the study abroad program at the Japan University of International Studies. Today, I am here to discuss the (1) _____ to take when you encounter an emergency situation in Japan. As you probably know, Japan is an earthquake-(2) _____ country. Let's discuss what to do before, during, and after an earthquake.

First, in your daily life, prepare an emergency bag. In your bag, keep a flashlight, emergency food, drinking water, a copy of your passport, and extra clothes. The website that I'm showing right now gives you more suggestions about what to have ready. Also, check where you should (3) _____ to. For example, our university's evacuation spot is the central lawn.

Next, what to do during the earthquake. As this website shows, DROP to the ground. It will help you from falling over when the ground is shaking. Also, COVER yourself, especially your head and neck. If possible, you should also HOLD onto something (4) _____ until the earthquake is over.

Finally, what to do after an earthquake. If you are in your house, make sure the gas is off. When you evacuate, avoid using the elevator. Another important issue is information. Make sure you collect (5) _____ information by yourself. Listen to TV and radio announcements, instead of information on social media. Don't be (6) _____ by fake news. An example of such a (7) _____ could be "I heard that a town nearby is (8) _____ because of earthquake-related fires and (9) _____ (10) _____." Decide by yourself if the information is coming from a legitimate source. Also, do not re-tweet these rumors to avoid confusion.

Speaking outline: *Cause and effect* 🎧 1-33

Suggest one thing you should avoid for your safety. Explain what problems this may cause.

1) Introduction	Imagine that _____.
2) Cause	In such a situation, one of the things you need to avoid is _____.
2) Effect	Otherwise, you would end up with _____. There would also be a problem with _____.
3) Conclusion	In conclusion, to prepare for an emergency, you need _____.

Gender

社会的性差について考えよう

Warm-up: *Share your ideas.*

Think of a typical family with little children. Which of the parents work?

a. The father works full-time.

b. The mother works full-time.

c. Both parents work full-time.

d. Both parents work part-time.

> *I chose answer _____, because...*
> ....
> ....
> ....

Words in focus: *Search the internet for words and phrases.*

 1-34

❏ colleague

❏ complaint

❏ contract

❏ groping

❏ miss each other

❏ peak hours

❏ politician

❏ retire

❏ segregation

❏ sexual assault

Dialogue

■ *Your mom sounds really great!*

1. Listen to each phrase, and guess what the speaker implies.

🔊 1-35

1. (　　) | (A) Fathers generally earn the most money.
2. (　　) | (B) The office had business in Japan.
3. (　　) | (C) He started work in another office.

2. Listen to the conversation and fill in the blanks.

🔊 1-36, 37

Mari is talking to Jack, her friend from Ireland.

<Scene 1>

Mari: So Jack, how did you get interested in Japan?

Jack: Well, I first lived here for a year as a child.

Mari: Oh, why was that?

Jack: My mum's company asked her to come and do some work over here, so we all came along.

Mari: Your mom?

Jack: Yeah, that's right. (1) _____

_____ and she had lots of things to do over here.

Mari: So you all came with her?

Jack: Yeah. My dad took a break for one year so that we could all come to Japan together.

Mari: That's cool!

<Scene 2>

Jack: Yeah, we all had a great time in Japan. I can't forget the steak we used to eat on family birthdays!

Mari: Your mom sounds really great, Jack. (2) _____

_____

Jack: Does your mum work, Mari?

Mari: Yes, she has a job in a local restaurant. She just works at lunchtime. Dad works so late every day!

Jack: So do you see your dad after he gets home?

Mari: No. Actually, we aren't living together.

Jack: Oh, I see.

Mari: My dad works far away, near Tokyo. (3) _____

_____ a few years ago, but we stayed in Kansai.

3. Listen to the conversation again and choose the best answer to each question. (repeat) 1-36, 37

\<Scene 1\> Why did Jack first visit Japan?

   (A) He worked for a Japanese company.

   (B) He was interested in Japan.

   (C) His father needed a rest.

   (D) His mother had work in Japan.

\<Scene 2\> What does Mari's mother do?

   (A) She celebrates Jack's birthday.

   (B) She works part-time.

   (C) She works late at night.

   (D) She works in Tokyo.

4. Listen to scenes 3 to 5, and choose the best answer to each question. 1-38, 39, 40

\<Scene 3\> Why didn't Mari's family move to Tokyo with her father?

   (A) Because of her mother's job.

   (B) Because her father would be too busy.

   (C) Because of Mari's school.

   (D) Because her mother dislikes Tokyo.

\<Scene 4\> Which is NOT a reason for Mari's father to stay in Tokyo on weekends?

   (A) He has to work on Saturdays.

   (B) He doesn't have the energy to go home.

   (C) He has to go out with colleagues at night.

   (D) He has to prepare dinner for Mari.

\<Scene 5\> What is Jack surprised about?

   (A) Mari's parents both working full time.

   (B) Mari cooking dinner.

   (C) Mari's family living apart.

   (D) Mari's father retiring soon.

Viewpoints

(repeat) 🎵 1-36, 37, 38, 39, 40

マリとジャックの会話から日本とアイルランドの家族像の違いが表れているフレーズをもう一度聞き、書き取りましょう。

<Scene 1> ジャックの父親	Jack: My _d___ took a _br_____ for _o_ _y____ so that we could _a__ _c_____ to _J_____ _t_____.
<Scene 2> マリの父親	Mari: His _c_____ _tr_____ him a _f_ _y____ _a__, but we _st_____ in _K_____.
<Scene 3> 子供の教育	Mari: My _p_____ _d_____ _w____ to _i_____ my _st_____.
<Scene 4> 両親の役割	Jack: Well, my _m___ was _a_____ the _m_ _e_____ in my _f_____. _D_ _w_____ too, but he was _u_____ the _f___o___ to _g___h____ and _p_____ _d_____ _f____u____.
<Scene 5> 夫婦の時間	Jack: I _h_____ your _p_____ can _e____ _d____ _m____ _t_____ _t_____ _a_____ _t____.

Pronunciation: *Rhythm* （リズム）

🎵 1-41

マリとジャックの会話の中で "company" という語が何度か出てきます。カタカナ日本語としての「カ・ン・パ・ニ・ー」とは発音がずいぶん異なります。このことには、ことばのリズムの取り方が日本語と英語で異なるということが関係しています。

● 日本語では基本的に「カ・ン・パ・ニ・ー」のように1文字ずつをほぼ等間隔で拍を取りますが、英語の "cóm·pa·ny" には3音節しかありません。

● 日本語では「カンパニー」のように「カ」の部分が高くなりますが、英語でcompanyと言うときには「cóm·pa·ny」のように「cóm」の部分が強く高く長く、残りの「pa」と「ny」の部分は弱く短く発音されます。

以下の単語の発音をもう一度聞いて、カタカナ発音との違いを確認しましょう。

Ja·pán   cón·tract   to·**géth·**er   **fám·**i·ly   **rés·**tau·rant

Monologue

■ *Women-only train cars.*

1. Choose the phrase that is related to each word, and practice reading it out loud. 🎧 1-42

1. blind	( )	**(a)** a person traveling in a vehicle
2. complaint	( )	**(b)** a dialect spoken in a region
3. effective	( )	**(c)** an act such as rape
4. groping	( )	**(d)** negative comment
5. local language	( )	**(e)** out of date
6. old-fashioned	( )	**(f)** separation of one group of people from another
7. passenger	( )	**(g)** successful
8. prevent	( )	**(h)** to stop, decrease
9. segregation	( )	**(i)** unable to see
10. sexual assault	( )	**(j)** illegally touching other people's sensitive body parts

2. Listen to the monologue and choose the best answer to each question. 🎧 1-43

1. Which of these is the basis for supporting women-only cars?

  (A) Both men and women can ride when it is crowded.

  (B) Many cases of groping are reported every year.

  (C) Everyone agrees with this idea.

  (D) There is no law prohibiting men from these cars.

2. Which of these is evidence against women-only cars?

  (A) These cars are good for blind people.

  (B) Other cars may become more crowded.

  (C) These cars are an effective means of allowing sexual assault.

  (D) Politicians are making a safer society.

3. Which information is included in the sign but NOT mentioned in the lecture?

  (A) The car rules.

  (B) Exceptions to the rule.

  (C) The reason for the rule.

  (D) Data to support the reason.

WOMEN ONLY CAR

Help to reduce sexual assault on our trains!
Over 300 cases reported in 2019.
Children under the age of 12 may ride with a guardian.

STOP

3. Listen again and fill in the blanks with suitable forms of words in the previous page.

You are attending a university lecture on gender studies.   (repeat) 🎧 1-43

Okay, class, today's topic is how we can decrease the number of (1) _____ cases. I will give you one example: women-only cars. In Japan, crimes such as (2) _____ on crowded trains are not a rare problem. In fact, there are around 300-500 cases reported per year. To avoid such crimes, some train companies provide women-only cars. Men cannot ride these cars during peak hours. However, not everyone agrees with this idea.

One problem is that it is not clear whether these cars succeed at reducing groping. In Japan, there is no law against men getting on to women-only cars. We also need to consider (3) _____ who can't understand the system. For example, (4) _____ people cannot read the signs. There are people who cannot read the (5) _____. Also, mixed-sex cars can become more crowded as a result of the women-only cars.

Furthermore, there are many people who disagree that women-only train cars are an (6) _____ measure against sexual assault. When Germany introduced single-sex cars, one United Nations adviser said that it is more important for politicians to make a safer society. This means a place where women and men can live easily together. Other (7) _____ suggested that the measures were too (8) _____ and would not make any improvements to society.

What is really needed is a way of (9) _____ those crimes. (10) _____ should not be the only solution. In this class, I would like you to discuss the wider problems in society, and suggest how they can be dealt with. Now, I will give you 20 minutes to search for information on the internet. Then, we will start the discussion. Any questions?

Speaking outline: *Understanding timelines*   🎧 1-44

The roles of men and women are changing with the times. Take one country/region and explain how their customs/laws/ideas have changed.

1) Introduction	In this presentation, I will talk about how gender awareness has changed over time in _____.
2) Timeline	In the old days, _____. For example, _____. Nowadays, _____. We can say that _____. In the future, I think _____.
3) Conclusion	The history of gender awareness in _____ tells us that _____, because _____.

Religion

世界の宗教について考えよう

Warm-up: *Share your ideas.*

Which annual event is most important for you?

a. New Year's Eve/Day

b. Valentine's Day

c. Summer festivals

d. Christmas

I chose answer _____, because...

Words in focus: *Search the internet for words and phrases.*

 1-45

❑ ancestor

❑ bland

❑ Buddhist grave

❑ Islamic faith

❑ Jewish

❑ kosher

❑ shellfish-free

❑ spice

❑ vegan

❑ vegetarian

■ *Can you enjoy* bon odori?

1. Listen to each phrase, and guess what the speaker implies. 🎧 1-46

1. ( )	(A) Watch out for creatures in the sea.
2. ( )	(B) It is a traditional religious event.
3. ( )	(C) We welcome ancestors back to this world.

2. Listen to the conversation and fill in the blanks. 🎧 1-47, 48

Ken is talking with Ruby, a student from New Zealand.

<Scene 1>

Ruby: I can't wait to visit your hometown, Ken. Erm, what was it called again?

Ken: My grandparents are in Tokushima, Ruby. It'll be hot there in August!

Ruby: That's okay. I love going to the beach when it's hot. Are the beaches nice there?

Ken: Yes, but (1) _____

Ruby: Okay. I'll look out for them.

Ken: Actually, we have a lot more to do. You know the *Bon* festival, right?

Ruby: *Bon* festival? I'm not sure, what's that?

Ken: Well, it's a traditional Japanese festival. (2) _____

_____

<Scene 2>

Ruby: So, it's a kind of memorial for the dead?

Ken: Yes, that's right. (3) _____

Ruby: Oh. I see. I'm not sure if I should go.

Ken: You're Jewish, aren't you Ruby? So you can learn about a different religion.

Ruby: Right. But I'm not supposed to join other religious events.

Ken: Oh, it's not seriously religious. They have a huge street dance.

Ruby: Dancing in the street?

3. Listen to the conversation again and choose the best answer to each question.   (repeat) 🎵 1-47, 48

<Scene 1> What are Ken and Ruby planning to do together?

(A) Visit Ruby's parents.

(B) Go to Tokushima.

(C) Look for fish in the sea.

(D) Meet their ancestors.

<Scene 2> Which religions do Ruby and Ken belong to?

(A) Ken is Jewish, and Ruby can be Buddhist.

(B) Ruby is Jewish, and Ken can be Buddhist.

(C) Ken is Christian, and Ruby has no religion.

(D) Ruby is Christian, and Ken has no religion.

4. Listen to scenes 3 to 5, and choose the best answer to each question.   🎵 1-49, 50, 51

<Scene 3> What would Ruby like to do in Japan?

(A) Watch a religious event.

(B) Join a dance.

(C) Meet Ken's relatives.

(D) Experience a historical festival.

<Scene 4> Why can't Ruby join certain events in Japan?

(A) Because she will be at the beach.

(B) Because it will be too hot.

(C) Because she has no religion.

(D) Because of her religious beliefs.

<Scene 5> Which of these can Ruby do?

(A) Dance in *Bon Odori*.

(B) Visit Ken's family grave.

(C) Eat non kosher food.

(D) Meet Ken's family.

ケンとルビーの宗教に対する姿勢の違いが表れているフレーズをもう一度聞き、書き取りましょう。

\<Scene 1\> 盆祭り	**Ruby:** Bon festival? I'm _n___ s_____, _w_____ t_____? **Ken:** _F_____ m____ to h_____ the s_____ of our _a_____.
\<Scene 2\> 異教の行事	**Ruby:** But I'm _n__ s_____ to _j____ o____ r_____ e_____. **Ken:** Oh, it's _n__ s_____ r_____.
\<Scene 3\> 仏教	**Ruby:** I'm _s_____, Ken, but I _f____ u_____ _j_____ a _B_____ e_____. **Ken:** Well, _l__ me _k_____ if you _ch_____ your _m____.
\<Scene 4\> 墓参り	**Ruby:** So it's a Buddhist grave? **Ken:** _J___ a _tr_____ _J_____ f____ _gr_____. **Ruby:** Ken, I _c_____ g____ to a _B_____ _gr____.
\<Scene 5\> 食べ物	**Ken:** Oh _w_____, _c___ you _e__ t_____? **Ruby:** Well, _o_____ if they are _k_____.

Pronunciation: *Intonation*（抑揚）・ニュージーランド英語 🎧 1-52

以下のルビーの発話をもう一度聞いて、音の高さの変化を確かめましょう。これら4つの文はすべて上昇調で発話されていますが、それぞれ、ニュアンスが異なります。

● I can't wait to visit your hometown →, Ken ↗.（呼びかけ）

● Erm →, what was it called again ↗?（再確認のための wh 疑問文）

● That's okay ↗.（相手の同意を求める軽い説得？）

● Are the beaches nice there ↗?（疑問文）

一般的に、肯定文は下降調、yes-no 疑問文は上昇調、wh 疑問文などは下降調のイントネーションになると言われていますが、文脈によって、さまざまなイントネーションが使われます。

さらに、イントネーションには地域性があります。例えばニュージーランド英語では肯定文であっても文末が上昇する傾向があると言われています。上記の "That's okay ↗." の文末が上昇しているのも、ケンに同意を求めたのではなくニュージーランド英語らしさの表れかもしれません。

Monologue

■ *Don't give passengers the wrong in-flight meal!*

1. Choose the phrase that is related to each word, and practice reading it out loud. 🎧 1-53

1. bland	( )	**(a)** without care for other people
2. consequences	( )	**(b)** variety
3. disrespectful	( )	**(c)** food prepared according to Jewish requirements
4. faith	( )	**(d)** flour which is used to make bread
5. kosher	( )	**(e)** a diet which does not use any animal products
6. range	( )	**(f)** belief or religion
7. religious	( )	**(g)** believing in a religion such as Christianity
8. upset	( )	**(h)** simple, boring
9. vegan	( )	**(i)** results
10. wheat	( )	**(j)** disappointed, angry

2. Listen to the monologue and choose the best answer to each question. 🎧 1-54

1. What is the speaker's main argument?

   (A) Some children are very religious.

   (B) Social media reports are a big problem.

   (C) It is important to serve the right meals.

   (D) The airline food system is very simple.

2. What might happen if a passenger with an allergy is given the wrong meal?

   (A) The speaker will be upset.

   (B) The flight attendant will be sick.

   (C) The passenger could die.

   (D) The passenger could eat a bland meal.

3. Look at the menu card. Which is NOT suitable for Muslims?

   (A) Shellfish-free seafood pasta.

   (B) Vegetarian rice.

   (C) Kosher beef curry.

   (D) Bland lightly-salted pork.

GLOBAL AIR
In-flight menu

Passengers with dietary restrictions may order from the following alternatives:

Menu Contains

- *Shellfish-free seafood pasta*, with extra white fish and no shrimp
- *Vegetarian rice*, with kidney beans
- *Kosher beef curry*, based on traditional Jewish recipe
- *Bland lightly-salted pork*, with boiled vegetables

3. Listen again and fill in the blanks with suitable forms of words in the previous page.

You are listening to an explanation about in-flight meals for special passengers. (repeat) 🔊 1-54

Global Air is known for quality in-flight meals. One reason is that we offer a (1) _____ of meals to passengers with different needs. Yesterday, we heard how important it is to serve the right meals to children, vegetarian, and (2) _____ customers. Today, let me explain more of our special in-flight meals.

We carefully prepare food for our guests with food allergies. Common allergies are peanuts, shellfish, and (3) _____. Our passengers are promised a safe meal. When flying, it is difficult to provide medical care. In the worst case, passengers may die if given the wrong meal. Therefore, it's very important to check that each guest with Global Air is given an enjoyable meal which they can eat safely.

There are also many (4) _____ passengers who choose to fly with us but are unable to eat certain dishes. It's extremely (5) _____ to serve beef products to a member of the Hindu religion. People of Islamic (6) _____ cannot eat pork. Jewish people will only eat (7) _____ foods cooked in the right way. Meals are carefully prepared with stickers showing meal type, seat number, and name. However, if you make a mistake, passengers could be very (8) _____ and they might never forgive us. They will also write about their bad experiences on social media sites. Very quickly, large groups of people will stop travelling with us.

Did I tell you we also offer a meal option called "(9) _____"? This means that the dish contains simple ingredients and no spice. Passengers who order bland meals may be upset, too, if we serve the wrong dish. The system is simple, but please understand the (10) _____ of making a mistake. You can ask me now if you have any questions.

Speaking outline: *Similarities and differences*

🔊 1-55

Find two religious events and describe a similarity and a difference between them. What do you recommend others to do?

1) Introduction	I am going to introduce _____ and _____. There are similarities and differences between them.
2) Similarity	One thing that _____ and _____ have in common is _____. For example, _____.
3) Difference	On the other hand, they are different in _____. For example, _____.
4) Conclusion	I would recommend you to be aware that _____.

Business

Warm-up: *Share your ideas.*

What do you want to keep in mind most when you start working?

a. Contribute to the profits of the company.

b. Make friends with your colleagues.

c. Not to hurt your boss's feelings.

d. Respect international perspectives.

I chose answer _____, because...

Words in focus: *Search the internet for words and phrases.*

 1-56

❏ agenda

❏ brainstorming

❏ corporate tax

❏ government agency

❏ IPOS

❏ IRAS

❏ launch

❏ multiethnic society

❏ patent

❏ strategy

Dialogue

■ *Business manners and etiquette in Singapore.*

1. Listen to each phrase, and guess what the speaker implies.   🎧 1-57

   1. (   ) | (A) I may not be able to adapt to a new environment.

   2. (   ) | (B) Let's have a coffee together.

   3. (   ) | (C) What are you carrying?

2. Listen to the conversation and fill in the blanks.   🎧 1-58, 59

Mari is talking with Dave, an international student from Singapore.

<Scene 1>

Mari: Hey, Dave. Where are you going?

Dave: I'm gonna grab a cup of coffee at my favorite cafe around the corner. (1) _____

_____

Mari: This is a welcome packet from the international internship program.

Dave: Wow! You got accepted? Congratulations!

Mari: Thanks!

Dave: Where are you going to work?

Mari: I am going to Singapore next month.

Dave: Fantastic! Have you ever been there?

Mari: No, never. I'm so excited but at the same time, a bit nervous.

<Scene 2>

Dave: How come?

Mari: (2) _____

So, what is it like in Singapore?

Dave: Well, unlike Japan, Singapore is a diverse society. The majority of the population in business is Chinese, followed by Malays and Indians.

Mari: I didn't know that Singapore was such a multi-ethnic society. That makes me more nervous.

Dave: Don't worry. If you have common sense, you should be fine in global business.

Mari: Common sense in Singapore may be different from what I think it is.

Dave: Well, I can give you some tips.

Mari: Thanks, Dave, that's what I expected. (3) _____

_____

Dave: Sounds good.

3. Listen to the conversation again and choose the best answer to each question. (repeat) 🎧 1-58, 59

<Scene 1> Why is Mari going to Singapore?

(A) To meet Dave.

(B) To buy coffee.

(C) To do an internship.

(D) To buy an envelope.

<Scene 2> Why does Mari want coffee?

(A) Because she wants to talk more with Dave.

(B) Because she is nervous.

(C) Because Dave is drinking one.

(D) Because Dave wants a break.

4. Listen to scenes 3 to 5, and choose the best answer to each question. 🎧 1-60, 61, 62

<Scene 3> What do Mari and Dave NOT mention as an inappropriate topic?

(A) Facial features.

(B) Racial groups.

(C) Money.

(D) Rumors.

<Scene 4> What does Dave say about Singaporeans?

(A) They are mean to people.

(B) They are hard to get along with.

(C) They are good at keeping time.

(D) They like Japanese people.

<Scene 5> What does Dave suggest about arranging a lunch meeting in Singapore?

(A) Plan the meeting after work.

(B) Search for restaurants with diverse food options.

(C) Order lots of alcoholic drinks.

(D) Order pork and beef.

マリとデイブの会話から、シンガポールと日本の共通点と相違点が表れているフレーズをもう一度聞き、書き取りましょう。

\<Scene 2\> 相違点	**Dave:**	Well, unlike _J_____, _S_____ is a _d_____ _s_____.
\<Scene 2\> 共通点	**Dave:**	If you _h____ c_____ s_____, you should be _f_____ in _g_____ b_____.
\<Scene 3\> 共通点	**Mari:** **Dave:**	_I_____ t_____? Like _r_____, r_____, and _p_____? Yes, as well as _p_____ a_____ and _g_____.
\<Scene 4\> 共通点	**Dave:**	_S_____ are _p_____.
\<Scene 5\> 相違点	**Dave:** **Mari:**	_S_____ p_____ a p_____ l_____ instead of having _d_____ with _c_____ or _cl_____. So, I should _f_____ a r_____ that can _s_____ a m_____ for them.

以下のマリの発話では、単語の終わりにある子音と、次の単語の最初にある母音がつながって聞こえます。「 _ 」の記号でつながっている単語の発音を聞いてみましょう。

● This_is_a welcome packet from the international_internship program.

● I am worried_if_I can fit_into a different culture.

● So, what_is_it like_in Singapore?

一方、デイブの発話では単語の終わりにある子音が聞こえにくくなっています。これはシンガポール英語でよく起こると言われている現象です。{ 波カッコ } で示されている子音に注目して聞いてみましょう。

● Wha{t} is tha(t) bi{g} envelo{pe} in your han{d}?

● You go{t} accep{ted}?

(丸カッコ) で示されている tha(t) の語末については Unit 8 を参照してください。

Monologue

EC

■ *Launching an import business in Singapore.*

1. Choose the phrase that is related to each word, and practice reading it out loud. 🔵 CD 1-64

1. act	( )	**(a)** a rule made by any organization
2. agenda	( )	**(b)** a list of matters to be discussed at a meeting
3. corporate	( )	**(c)** a law that has been passed by a parliament
4. impose	( )	**(d)** exactly or correctly
5. inland	( )	**(e)** money that a government receives
6. launch	( )	**(f)** relating to a business
7. patent	( )	**(g)** the official legal right to make or sell an invention
8. regulation	( )	**(h)** to begin something
9. revenue	( )	**(i)** to officially force
10. strictly	( )	**(j)** within the borders of a country

2. Listen to the monologue and choose the best answer to each question. 🔵 CD 1-65

1. What is the main purpose of the talk?

(A) To build a marketing strategy.

(B) To plan a trip to Singapore.

(C) To make their business website.

(D) To change regulations.

2. What are the participants likely to do in the next 10 minutes?

(A) Launch an import business in Singapore.

(B) Take a break.

(C) Change the tax system in Singapore.

(D) Visit the website to find today's agenda.

3. The figure shows the corporate tax rate in Singapore for different years.
In which year(s) was the tax rate higher than in 2010?

(A) 1997-2000.

(B) 2002.

(C) 2007-2009.

(D) All of the above.

Year	Corporate tax rate
1997-2000	26.0%
2001	25.5%
2002	24.5%
2003-2004	22.0%
2005-2006	20.0%
2007-2009	18.0%

出典：Hawksford（2008）.
Singapore Corporate Tax Guide
https://www.guidemesingapore.com/business-guides/
taxation-and-accounting/corporate-tax/singapore-
corporate-tax-guide

3. Listen again and fill in the blanks with suitable forms of words in the previous page.

You are attending a business meeting at an import company in Singapore. (repeat) 🔊 1-65

Good morning. Let me pass out a copy of the (1) _____. As you know, we are
(2) _____ an import business here in Singapore next year. Today is the first meeting for
building a marketing strategy. So, I will talk about government guidelines we should keep in
mind. These are the tax system, intellectual property protection, and import (3) _____.
After that, we will do some brainstorming for the marketing strategy together. Shall we start?

Let's begin with the tax system. The (4) _____ (5) _____ Authority of
Singapore, or IRAS, is the government agency that is in charge of the tax system. Both local
and foreign companies have (6) _____ taxes (7) _____ on them. The current tax rate
of 17% took effect in 2010. The length of the financial year is 12 months.

Next, I will talk about the agency of intellectual property protection. The Intellectual
Property Office of Singapore, or IPOS, manages intellectual property rights such as
(8) _____, copyrights, or trademarks. As far as I know, the agency enforces the law
(9) _____, so it works well. You can find the URL of the IPOS on page 3 of the agenda.

The last topic is import regulations. One of the regulations I want you to know is the
Customs (10) _____. I will deliver a regulation handbook to each of you this afternoon,
so please read it through by the next meeting.

So far so good? I know I gave you too much information, so some of you might be a bit
confused. Why don't we have a 10-minute break to clear our heads?

Speaking outline: *Categorization*   🔊 1-66

Find some companies that operate across national borders. Which of the following categories
do they fall under?

international / transnational / multinational companies

importing / exporting / licensing / franchising / foreign direct investment / outsourcing

1) Introduction	The companies I did research on are _____ and _____. You often hear the names of these companies, but did you know how they do business?
2) Categorization	First, _____ is a(n) _____ corporation. They first started as _____. Now, they mainly do business in the area of _____. Secondly, _____ is a(n) _____ corporation. They _____.
3) Conclusion	In sum, there are different types of businesses in the world. I found it interesting that _____.

Career

キャリア形成について考えよう

Warm-up: *Share your ideas.*

What is most important for your career development?

a. Stable employment conditions.

b. Chances to demonstrate your potential.

c. Experiences for future employment.

d. Work-life balance.

I chose answer _____, because...

....

....

....

Words in focus: *Search the internet for words and phrases.*

 2-01

❑ be qualified

❑ conformity

❑ cooperativeness

❑ CV, résumé

❑ e-commerce company

❑ hospitality business

❑ job candidate

❑ negotiation skills

❑ recruiter

❑ self-analysis

Dialogue

■ *How can I make the most of my strengths?*

1. Listen to each phrase, and guess what the speaker implies.   CD 2-02

   1. (   )   (A) They must be having a hard time.

   2. (   )   (B) I like the way you look now.

   3. (   )   (C) All the people were wearing formal clothes.

2. Listen to the conversation and fill in the blanks.   CD 2-03, 04

Ken is talking with Asha, an international student from India.

\<Scene 1\>

   Ken: Hi, Asha. I saw you at the job seminar this morning.

   Asha: Oh, hi, Ken. Were you there, too? Sorry, I didn't notice

   you because (1) _____

   _____

   Ken: It's okay. I found you there because you were the only person in a red sweatshirt.

   You look good in red, but we usually wear suits in seminars like that.

   Asha: Right. It was a surprise!

   Ken: Well, it's no surprise. Everyone wears suits while job hunting.

   Asha: But (2) _____ It must be hard

   to identify students in the same outfit.

\<Scene 2\>

   Ken: I've never thought about that. I suppose the dark suits are meant to show conformity

   and cooperativeness.

   Asha: You're right. I got that during the latter half of the seminar.

   Ken: Actually, I left the room in the middle of the seminar. Was it good?

   Asha: There was a make-up course for female students only.

   Ken: Only for female students?

   Asha: Yes. They told us what colour our cheeks should be.

   Ken: Who told you that?

   Asha: A lady from a cosmetics company instructed us on how to apply blusher. But my skin

   won't look like a Japanese student's.

   Ken: Don't worry. (3) _____

3. Listen to the conversation again and choose the best answer to each question. (repeat) 2-03, 04

<Scene 1> Why does Asha feel sorry for recruiters?

(A) Because they cannot wear red clothes.

(B) Because they must attend the seminar.

(C) Because they cannot find a specific student.

(D) Because they must be tired.

<Scene 2> What is NOT true about the make-up seminar?

(A) It was taught in the latter part of the seminar.

(B) Students were not allowed to leave the room.

(C) Students were told to use a certain color for their cheeks.

(D) It was taught by a female instructor.

4. Listen to scenes 3 to 5, and choose the best answer to each question. 2-05, 06, 07

<Scene 3> Why did Ken leave halfway through the seminar?

(A) Because he needed to fix his make-up.

(B) Because he wanted to find work abroad.

(C) Because he didn't find any e-commerce companies on the list.

(D) Because he was told to start his own company.

<Scene 4> Which of the following is true about Asha?

(A) She has already decided on her future job.

(B) She wants to work outside Japan.

(C) She is bilingual.

(D) She is writing Ken's résumé.

<Scene 5> What did Asha suggest Ken should do?

(A) Work in a Japanese company.

(B) Expect the company to help him.

(C) Show how he can contribute to the company.

(D) Emphasize that he can speak English.

Viewpoints

repeat 2-03, 04, 05, 06, 07

就職活動についてケンとアシャの捉え方の違いが表れているフレーズをもう一度聞き、書き取りましょう。

<Scene 1> リクルート スーツ	Ken: Well, it's _n_ _s_____. _E_____ _w_____ _s_____ while _j___ _h_____._ Asha: It _m_____ be _h____ to _i_____ _st_____ in the _s_____ _o_____.
<Scene 2> 就活メイク	Asha: But my _s___ _w____ _l____ like a _J_____ _s_____. Ken: _D____ _w____. I _th___ you _l___ _g____ as _y___ _a__.
<Scene 3> 将来設計	Ken: I want to _st____ my _o___ _e-_____ _c_____. Asha: You _c___ do _th___ in _J_____, _t__, _c____ _y___?
<Scene 4> 自己分析	Asha: I'm still _tr_____ to _f_____ out _h___ I can _m_____ the _m_____ of my _st_____ in _J_____ _c_____. Ken: _W___ _d___ we _h___ _e____ _o_____ to _w____ our _r_____?
<Scene 5> 企業への 貢献	Ken: I want to _l_____ _wh_____ they would _t_____ me. Asha: _W___ _c___ _y___ _d__ for them?

Pronunciation: *Weak form*（弱形）・インド英語

2-08

文の中で強勢が置かれない語が弱形で発音されると、聞き取りにくくなります。
以下の文で、[角括弧]で示した語が弱形で発音されていることを確認しましょう。

● I found [you] there [because] you were the only person in a red sweatshirt.
　　　[you] 強 /juː/ 弱 /ju/　　[because] 強 /bɪkʌz, -kɔ́ːz, -kɑ́ːz/ 弱 /kəz/

一方アシャの発話では、ほとんどの音節が弱化していないため忙しそうに聞こえるかもしれません。インド英語のイントネーションや発音にも注目しましょう。

● [But] I feel sorry [for] the recruiters.
　 [but] 強 /bʌt/ 弱 /bət/　 [for] 強 /fɔːr/ 弱 /fər/

● It [must] [be] hard [to] identify students in the same outfit.
　　　[must] 強 /mʌst/ 弱 /məs(t)/　　[be] 強 /biː/ 弱 /bi/　　[to] 強 /tuː/ 弱 /tə/

Monologue

What do the recruiters want to know?

1. Choose the phrase that is related to each word, and practice reading it out loud. 2-09

1. acquire ( )	**(a)** a group of businesses such as hotels and restaurants
2. athlete ( )	**(b)** a meeting for sharing information or instructions
3. briefing ( )	**(c)** a person who is competing to get a job
4. candidate ( )	**(d)** a person who is very good at sports
5. emphasize / emphasise ( )	**(e)** a written statement explaining your background
6. hospitality ( )	**(f)** enough for a particular purpose
7. initial ( )	**(g)** of or at the beginning
8. negotiation ( )	**(h)** discussing something to reach an agreement
9. résumé / CV ( )	**(i)** to get something
10. sufficient ( )	**(j)** to show that something is very important

2. Listen to the monologue and choose the best answer to each question. 2-10

1. Who is the speaker talking to?

    (A) New candidates for the job.

    (B) People who will interview candidates.

    (C) A student from the United States.

    (D) An athlete who wants to participate in competitions.

2. What does the speaker want to know about Candidate C?

    (A) When she played tennis.

    (B) If she has the team spirit.

    (C) How long she was in the hospitality business.

    (D) What she has learned from her part-time job.

3. Look at the poster. According to the speaker, which candidate fits all three of the job requirements?

    (A) Candidate A.

    (B) Candidate B.

    (C) Candidate C.

    (D) None of the above.

HOTEL RECEPTIONIST

Applicants must have:
- ✓ Ability to cooperate with others
- ✓ Experience in hospitality
- ✓ A minimum of one year studying abroad

Email your CV to bhotel@vacancy.com

3. Listen again and fill in the blanks with suitable forms of words in the previous page.

(repeat) 🎧 2-10

Some recruiters are having a meeting before the final interview with job candidates.

Okay. Let's start the (1) _____ . Did you get all the documents ready? Good. As you see, the first interview is for three people. They are all newly graduated from university. The (2) _____ questions to ask all the (3) _____ are the same as usual. For the individual questions, I have some ideas.

First, candidate A. Her (4) _____ says, "gained communication skills through studying abroad for two months." Here, I want to know what she did during those two months. You know, just taking ESL classes may not be (5) _____ to give her enough experience to gain the (6) _____ skills required for this position. Let's ask her what she achieved in the US.

Next, a question for candidate B. He says, "(7) _____ the spirit of cooperation through a club activity." Let's find out what role he had in this tennis club. It seems that there are two types of clubs in Japanese universities. One is for (8) _____ who aim to participate in competitions. The other is more for socialising. I want to hear a story that shows evidence of the "team spirit" that he gained.

The last one. Candidate C (9) _____ her part-time job experience. She has been in the (10) _____ business for three years. I want to know what she has learnet from that experience. We also need to find out how she can apply those skills to her job in our company.

So these are my ideas for the individual questions. If you have any others, feel free to ask them. However, please make sure that you avoid the questions on the list. It is illegal to ask about some topics, so don't forget to check the list before you open your mouth.

Speaking outline: *Sequencing*

🎧 2-11

Imagine your future 20 years from now. What do you want/need to do in the next 20 years?

1) Introduction	I want to _____ in 20 years from now. Today, I will talk about what I want/need to do to achieve that goal.
2) Sequence	First, while in college, I _____ because _____ . Next, for a few years after graduation, I _____ . By doing so, the next 10 years will be _____ .
3) Conclusion	In summary, there will be three phases in my next 20 years, which are _____ , _____ , and _____ . I hope I can _____ .

Japanese Culture

日本の文化について考えよう

Warm-up: *Share your ideas.*

Which of the following are you most interested in when thinking about Japanese culture?

a. Art.

b. Language.

c. Lifestyle.

d. Ways of thinking.

I chose answer _____, because...
....
....
....

Words in focus: *Search the internet for words and phrases.* 2-12

❏ barrier

❏ cosmetic salting

❏ flexibility

❏ funeral

❏ grin

❏ honorific form

❏ Japanese celebration

❏ priority

❏ red sea bream

❏ sliding door

Dialogue

■ *Being polite, or being friendly?*

1. Listen to each phrase, and guess what the speaker implies.

🔵 CD 2-13

1. (   )
2. (   )
3. (   )

> (A) It seems you are not in a good mood.
> (B) I did not do it on purpose.
> (C) You may not have done anything wrong.

2. Listen to the conversation and fill in the blanks.

🔵 CD 2-14, 15

Mari is talking to Ivan from Russia, her co-worker at a convenience store.

<Scene 1>

Mari: Hey, Ivan, are you okay? (1) _____

Ivan: Me? No, not at all. I enjoy working with you here.

Mari: Oh, I thought you were angry because you never smile.

Ivan: Why do you want me to smile? There's nothing funny. You sometimes grin at me, but why don't you concentrate on your work?

<Scene 2>

Mari: I'm just trying to cheer you up because you are in such a bad mood. The other day you scared a customer away when she asked if we had nail polish.

Ivan: Nail polish? Yes, I remember her. I showed her where it was. Then, she decided not to buy anything and left the store. She seemed upset, but I wasn't.

Mari: Ivan, (2) _____, but it was the way you treated her. You didn't say a word and just pointed at the nail polish. You didn't even look at her. Why are you always so cold to the customers?

Ivan: (3) _____! That day I was organising the shelves in the store. She must have noticed that I was busy with my own work. I always try my best to get things done as quickly as possible.

3. Listen to the conversation again and choose the best answer to each question. (repeat) 🅒🅓 2-14, 15

<Scene 1> Why did Mari ask Ivan if he was okay?

      (A) Because he seemed to be angry.

      (B) Because he enjoyed working.

      (C) Because he grinned at Mari.

      (D) Because he kept on smiling.

<Scene 2> What does Ivan consider as a part of his job?

      (A) Becoming friends with the customers.

      (B) Creating a relaxing atmosphere.

      (C) Making customers feel tense.

      (D) Getting the job done quickly.

4. Listen to scenes 3 to 5, and choose the best answer to each question. 2-16, 17, 18

<Scene 3> What does Mari consider as a part of her job?

      (A) Becoming friends with the customers.

      (B) Creating a relaxing atmosphere.

      (C) Making customers feel tense.

      (D) None of the above.

<Scene 4> What did Ivan do after the interview?

      (A) He started to worry about Mari.

      (B) He began to get nervous.

      (C) He showed respect to the owner.

      (D) He memorized the phrases on the list.

<Scene 5> At the end of the conversation, what did Mari suggest Ivan do?

      (A) Be tense and unfriendly.

      (B) Be polite and friendly.

      (C) Stay polite, but not friendly.

      (D) Stay friendly, but not polite.

Viewpoints

(repeat) 2-14, 15, 16, 17, 18

マリとイヴァンの会話から顧客サービスの文化に対する考え方の違いが表れているフレーズをもう一度聞き、書き取りましょう。

<Scene 1> 笑顔	**Mari:**	Oh, I _th_____ you were _a_____ because you _n_____ s_____.
	Ivan:	You _s_____ g____ at me, but _w____ don't you _c_____ on your _w_____?
<Scene 2> 顧客対応	**Mari:**	Why are you _a_____ so _c_____ to the _c_____?
	Ivan:	She must have _n_____ that I was _b_____ with my _o____ _w_____.
<Scene 3> 親しみやすさ	**Mari:**	Can you be a _l_____ _m_____ _f_____?
	Ivan:	They do _n__ _e_____ me to be their _f_____.
<Scene 4> 緊張感	**Mari:**	Anyway, I am _w_____ about you because you _a_____ _l___ _t_____.
	Ivan:	Mm, I do _t___ to _l____ _p_____.
<Scene 5> 敬語	**Ivan:**	Also, the _h_____ _f_____ is used for _c_____ a _b_____ between the _s_____.
	Mari:	Oh, I've _n_____ _th_____ about that.

Pronunciation: *Dropping* （脱落）・ロシアの英語

 2-19

以下のマリの発話では (カッコ) で示されている音が脱落して聞こえなくなっています。特に、/p, t, k, b, d, g/ のような閉鎖音が子音の間に挟まれたときや、似た音がつながったときに聞こえにくくなります。

● I'm jus(t) trying to cheer you u(p) because you are in such a ba(d) mood.

イヴァンの発話でも脱落が起こっています。太字で示した /w/ の音にも注目しましょう。/w/ が /v/ のように聞こえるのは、ロシア英語の特徴のひとつです。

● **Wh**y do you **w**an(t) me to smile?

● You sometimes grin a(t) me, bu(t) **wh**y don't you concentra(te) on your **w**ork?

Monologue

■ *Left face!*

1. Choose the phrase that is related to each word, and practice reading it out loud. 🎧 2-20

1. celebration	( )	**(a)** a ceremony after someone dies
2. cosmetic	( )	**(b)** a happy event
3. flesh	( )	**(c)** a kind of fish
4. funeral	( )	**(d)** a part of the fish you can eat
5. grill	( )	**(e)** intended to improve the appearance
6. priority	( )	**(f)** something that is more important than others
7. raw	( )	**(g)** to become smaller
8. red sea bream	( )	**(h)** to consider
9. regard	( )	**(i)** to cook over a fire
10. shrink	( )	**(j)** without being cooked

2. Listen to the monologue and choose the best answer to each question. 🎧 2-21

1. What kind of fish is suitable for this recipe?

(A) *Tai*.

(B) Red sea breams.

(C) Snappers.

(D) Any of the above.

2. What is NOT mentioned as one of the three rules?

(A) Grill the fish instead of serving it raw.

(B) Cover the fragile parts with salt.

(C) Make a cross-cut on the surface of the fish.

(D) Dish up the fish with its head facing left.

3. Look at the graphic. Choose the correct description of Uncle Osamu's recipe.

(A) He bought the fish 40 minutes ago.

(B) This recipe was recommended by four chefs.

(C) All the ingredients were explained in his show.

(D) The fish is served according to the third rule.

Salt-Grilled Red Sea Bream (Tai-no-Sioyaki)
By Uncle Osamu ★★★★☆(20 ratings)

Prep:40 mins Serves 4
Cook:20 mins

— ingredients —
4 whole red sea breams
4 tbsp sea salt
1 lemon / lime
4 tbsp grated daikon radish

3. Listen again and fill in the blanks with suitable forms of words in the previous page.

You are watching Uncle Osamu's Cooking Show. (repeat) 🎵 2-21

Welcome to Uncle Osamu's Kitchen. Today, I will show you how to prepare food for Japanese (1) _____. Did you know that (2) _____ is considered a lucky fish in Japan? It's called *tai* in Japanese, and the sound *tai* is associated with a Japanese word that means "happy," "joyful," or "lucky." It's also (3) _____ as the king of fish.

I got these nice red sea breams just yesterday. They were so fresh that I could have served them (4) _____. But today I'll (5) _____ them as they are, from top to bottom, saving all their skin and fins. If you cannot get *tai*, any variety of sea bream or snapper will do. Before we start, remember three rules: plenty of salt, an X, and head to the left.

Okay, rule number one. Before you grill the fish, press salt into their tails and fins. Cover them completely with salt to keep them from burning. You need your skin protected in the heat, right? It's the same thing. In fact, this process is called (6) _____ salting.

Rule number two. Cut an "X" into the (7) _____ on either side of the fish. This will help with even cooking, and prevent the skin from (8) _____ and bursting. Yes, another cosmetic reason.

Finally, when you serve the fish, keep its head to the left. It's important because at (9) _____ we serve fish with their heads to the right. In traditional Japanese culture, the left side has (10) _____ over the right side. You find this left-priority tradition in kimonos, sliding doors, or seating arrangements.

Speaking outline: *Comparison and contrast*   🎵 2-22

Choose one culture that is different from the culture in Japan and compare them.

1) Introduction	In this presentation, I will compare _____ and Japanese culture. Especially, I will focus on _____.
2) Comparison 1	In Japan _____. For example, _____. In contrast, in _____, _____. An example is _____.
3) Comparison 2	Secondly, another example of Japanese culture is _____. On the other hand, in _____, _____. For instance, _____.
4) Conclusion	To summarize the results of the comparison, _____ and Japan differ in _____, _____, and _____.

Law and Peace

法と平和について考えよう

Warm-up: *Share your ideas.*

Which of the following are you most interested in to protect world peace?

a. Economic development.

b. Social justice.

c. Respect for human rights.

d. Security system.

I chose answer _____, because...

Words in focus: *Search the internet for words and phrases.* 2-23

❑ abolition of the death penalty

❑ counterattack

❑ heinous crime

❑ humanitarian

❑ international law

❑ IRGC

❑ JSDF

❑ the Charter of the United Nations

❑ US military base

❑ use of force

Dialogue

■ *War or use of force? Self-defense force is not armed?*

1. Listen to each phrase, and guess what the speaker implies. 🎧 2-24

1. (   )   (A) We must not hurt people.

2. (   )   (B) I knew about the case.

3. (   )   (C) I need to understand the content.

2. Listen to the conversation and fill in the blanks. 🎧 2-25, 26

Ken is talking with Sofia, a student in Brazil. Sofia is studying international law at graduate school.

<Scene 1>

   Ken: Sofia, I need your help with my homework, please.

Sofia: What is it?

   Ken: The topic is "Iran's Islamic Revolutionary Guard Corps
launching missiles against US troops in Iraq."

Sofia: That's a tough one. When is your homework due?

   Ken: (1) _____

Sofia: I see. (2) _____ It was in 2020.

   Ken: The Iranian military attacked the US military, right? But why?

Sofia: It was because an Iranian military leader was killed by a US drone strike.

   Ken: So Iran took revenge on the US. But why in Iraq?

Sofia: The US military bases were in Iraq.

<Scene 2>

   Ken: Why did the US stop dealing with it?

Sofia: The Iranian foreign minister concluded that they had taken proportionate measures
against the US.

   Ken: What does "proportionate" mean?

Sofia: It implies that Iran made the right amount of counterattacks against the US.

   Ken: So the US decided not to fight back?

Sofia: Well, I guess you can put it that way.

   Ken: I'm glad this war is over.

Sofia: Ken, didn't you study the definition of war under international law?

   Ken: Countries attacking each other, maybe? (3) _____

_____

3. Listen to the conversation again and choose the best answer to each question. (repeat)   2-25, 26

\<Scene 1\> What is the article about?

(A) US troops took revenge on Iran.

(B) Iran took revenge on US troops.

(C) A peace treaty was signed between the US and Iran.

(D) Iran gave a gift to the US.

\<Scene 2\> What is the "proportionate" use of force?

(A) To use it excessively to avoid danger.

(B) To use it accordingly with the type of danger.

(C) To use it experimentally in preparation for war.

(D) To use it regularly to threaten others.

4. Listen to scenes 3 to 5, and choose the best answer to each question. 2-27, 28, 29

\<Scene 3\> Which is true about Sofia's understanding of the Iranian strike?

(A) Iran started a war against the US.

(B) The US started a war against Iran.

(C) The strike should be considered as a war.

(D) The strike should be considered as a use of force.

\<Scene 4\> Why did Iran emphasize the "proportionate" use of force?

(A) To emphasize how powerful they are.

(B) To show that they acted in self-defense.

(C) To indicate that the US acted in self-defense.

(D) To announce that the Charter is wrong.

\<Scene 5\> Why did Ken deny that the JSDF is an armed force?

(A) Because he is confused about the term "self-defense."

(B) Because he is a trained soldier.

(C) Because he discussed it with Sophia.

(D) Because he did enough research.

ソフィアがケンに説明したことをもう一度聞き、書き取りましょう。

\<Scene 1\> イスラム革命 防衛隊による 攻撃	**Sofia:** It was in _20____. **Sofia:** It was because an _I_____ _m_____ _l_____ was _k_____ by a US _d_____ _s_____. **Sofia:** The US _m_____ _b_____ were in _I____.
\<Scene 2\> イランによる 声明	**Sofia:** It implies that _I____ made the _r_____ _a_____ of _c_____ against the _U_.
\<Scene 3\> 戦争の定義	**Sofia:** _W___ _b_____ with a _f_____ _d_____ of war by a _g_____. **Sofia:** So, it was "_u____ of _f_____" by _I____, not a _w___.
\<Scene 4\> 武力行使	**Sofia:** _S_____ _p__, all UN _M_____ _S_____ _sh_____ _r_____ from the _u__ of _f_____. **Sofia:** The _Ch_____ allows the use of force for _s____-_____.
\<Scene 5\> 日本の自衛隊	**Sofia:** Japan also has an _a_____ _f_____, right? **Sofia:** But the _J____ is _a_____, and it has _t_____ _s_____.

Pronunciation: *Assimilation*（同化）*1*・南米の英語　🔘 2-30

以下のケンの発話で、二重下線で示されている音を聞いてみましょう。隣り合った前後の音が混ざり合って別の音に変化する現象は「相互同化」と呼ばれます。

● Sofia, I nee<u>d y</u>our help with my homework, please.　　/d/ + /j/ → /dʒ/

相互同化は以下のような音の組み合わせでも起こります。ソフィアの発話を聞いてみましょう。

● When i<u>s y</u>our homework due?　　/z/ + /j/ → /ʒ/

● Well, I gues<u>s y</u>ou can put it that way.　　/s/ + /j/ → /ʃ/

● Ken, didn'<u>t y</u>ou study the definition of war under international law?　　/t/ + /j/ → /tʃ/

Monologue

■ *Is it a crime prevention measure, or an inhumane act?*

1. Choose the phrase that is related to each word, and practice reading it out loud. 2-31

1. abolition	( )	**(a)** cannot be avoided
2. criminal	( )	**(b)** death as a punishment
3. evidence	( )	**(c)** improving people's lives and reducing suffering
4. heinous	( )	**(d)** someone who has committed a crime
5. humanitarian	( )	**(e)** the act of officially ending something
6. irremediable	( )	**(f)** impossible to correct or cure
7. inevitable	( )	**(g)** a set of questions people are asked
8. inhumane	( )	**(h)** treating people in a cruel way
9. poll	( )	**(i)** very bad and shocking
10. capital punishment	( )	**(j)** something that makes you believe that something is true or exists

2. Listen to the monologue and choose the best answer to each question. 2-32

1. Who is supporting the death penalty?

(A) The moderator.

(B) The affirmative team.

(C) The opposing team.

(D) People in international society.

2. Look at the graph. What can be said about the affirmative team's argument?

(A) They showed data for the year with the highest ratio.

(B) They showed the oldest data.

(C) They showed the latest data at the time.

(D) They showed a yearly shift in the ratio.

3. Which is one of the reasons given by the opposing team?

(A) The Japanese government said it is unavoidable.

(B) The death penalty is banned in 56 countries.

(C) Abolishing the death penalty will increase crimes.

(D) Even if they are criminals, we should not kill people.

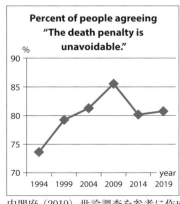

内閣府（2019）. 世論調査を参考に作成

53

3. Listen again and fill in the blanks with suitable forms of words in the previous page.

You are participating in debate competition training. (repeat) 2-32

> **Moderator:** Good afternoon, ladies and gentlemen. The topic for our debate today is "Should Japan keep its system of the death penalty or not?" Each team has one minute for the first argument. Affirmative team, you have the floor.

Affirmative Team:	Opposing Team:
Thank you, chair. We would like to emphasize that the death penalty is (1) _____. Now, we will be talking about the (2) _____. We will focus on public opinion, the safety of society, and (3) _____ grounds. First, an opinion (4) _____ by the Japanese government showed that 85 percent said its existence is "unavoidable." Second, the same poll showed that people are worried that the (5) _____ of the death penalty would lead to an increase in (6) _____ crimes. Third, family members of victims would not tolerate the fact that the (7) _____ continue to live their lives. They would expect the criminals to suffer from the same pain as them. In conclusion, we would like to emphasize that Japan should keep its system of the death penalty.	We disagree with the affirmative team. We will give you three reasons why the death penalty should be abolished. First, regarding public opinion, in fact, the death penalty is not common in international society. Only 56 countries and regions conduct (8) _____. Second, the results of a survey show that its abolition would not lead to an increase in heinous crimes. Third, killing a person is (9) _____ even as a penalty. Moreover, if there are errors during trials, they are (10) _____. We would like to conclude our argument insisting that the abolition of the death penalty is necessary.

Speaking outline: *Main idea and details (2)* 2-33

Should the war against terrorism be accepted in international law? Explain the terms "war" and "terrorism" in detail, and express your opinion.

1) Main idea	I think "the war against terrorism" should / should not be considered a war. I will start my presentation by quoting the definitions of "war" and "terrorism."
2) Detail 1	According to _____, "war" is defined as _____. That is to say, _____.
3) Detail 2	According to _____, "terrorism" is defined as _____. In other words, _____.
4) Your opinion	Therefore, _____.

Ethnicity

民族性について考えよう

Warm-up: *Share your ideas.*

Which issue is the most important to consider in a multi-ethnic society?

a. Ethnic conflict.

b. Endangered ethnic minority groups.

c. Integration into the majority ethnic group.

d. Respect for different cultures.

I chose answer _____, because...
....
....
....

Words in focus: *Search the internet for words and phrases.*

2-34

❑ ethnic diversity

❑ Han Chinese

❑ interracial marriage

❑ language policy

❑ Mandarin Chinese

❑ medium of instruction

❑ multi-ethnic children

❑ transformation of cultures

❑ trilingual

❑ vanishing cultures

Dialogue

■ *She did not have to feel sorry for me.*

1. Listen to each phrase, and guess what the speaker implies. 🎧 2-35

   1. (　　　)　　　(A) I don't know anything about it.

   2. (　　　)　　　(B) She was paying attention to me.

   3. (　　　)　　　(C) I don't worry about it anymore.

2. Listen to the conversation and fill in the blanks. 🎧 2-36, 37

Mari is talking to Eric, an international student from China.

<Scene 1>

  Mari: Hi, Eric. How was your class?

   Eric: I had Asian history. I usually enjoy it, but I felt

           uncomfortable today.

  Mari: What happened?

   Eric: When the professor was talking about history,

          (1) _____

  Mari: Because you are Chinese?

   Eric: I guess so, but she didn't have to feel sorry for me.

  Mari: Maybe she wanted to hear different points of view from you.

   Eric: So, I should have given some comments in class?

  Mari: That's what I think.

   Eric: I see. (2) _____

<Scene 2>

  Mari: That's good to hear. So, did you learn anything new?

   Eric: Well, did you know how many different ethnic groups there are in China?

  Mari: (3) _____

   Eric: There are more than 50 ethnic groups.

  Mari: That many?

   Eric: Yes. Han Chinese is the major ethnic group. It makes up about 90% of the population

          in China.

3. Listen to the conversation again and choose the best answer to each question. (repeat)  2-36, 37

<Scene 1> Why didn't Eric feel comfortable in class?

(A) Because he had no history class today.

(B) Because his teacher came from China.

(C) Because his teacher kept looking at him.

(D) Because he was not allowed to give comments.

<Scene 2> What does Eric tell Mari?

(A) Mari didn't learn anything new in her class.

(B) He didn't know how many people are in China.

(C) There are 50 students in his class.

(D) Most of the people in China belong to one ethnic group.

4. Listen to scenes 3 to 5, and choose the best answer to each question. 2-38, 39, 40

<Scene 3> What does Eric imply about China's language policy?

(A) 10% of the population speaks 50 languages.

(B) It is the right policy.

(C) Minority languages are taught in schools.

(D) Some people are not allowed to speak their own language.

<Scene 4> Which of the following was the discussion topic in Mari's class?

(A) The professor's self-introduction.

(B) The importance of language.

(C) English education at the university.

(D) Establishing a building plan.

<Scene 5> Which of the following is implied about Eric's parents?

(A) They are teachers.

(B) His father is Japanese.

(C) They like Mari's teacher.

(D) They speak three languages.

Viewpoints

マリとエリックが推測しながら話しているフレーズをもう一度聞き、書き取りましょう。

<Scene 1>先生の気持ち	**Mari:** B_____ you are Ch_____? **Eric:** I g_____ so, but she d_____ have to f___ s_____ for me. **Mari:** M_____ she w_____ to h___ d_____ p_____ of v_____ from you.
<Scene 2>中国の民族	**Mari:** I h____ n___ i_____. **Eric:** There are m_____ t_____ 50 e_____ g_____.
<Scene 3>中国の少数民族	**Mari:** Then, ___% of the p_____ in Ch_____ are d_____ into m_____ than ___ e_____ g_____. **Mari:** They m____ b___ p_____ of their c_____.
<Scene 4>言語の役割	**Mari:** L_____ is c_____ for k_____ your own c_____, r_____? **Eric:** A_____, doesn't it lead to e_____ your own i_____ and b_____ s____-c_____?
<Scene 5>マリの先生の両親	**Eric:** Oh, he is j_____ l_____ me, th_____.

Pronunciation: *Assimilation*（同化）*2*・中国の英語

ある音が、直前の音の影響を受けて別の音に変化する現象は順行同化、直後の音の影響を受けて変化する現象は逆行同化と呼ばれます。二重下線で示されている音を聞いてみましょう。

● That's what I think.
　　　/hwʌt aɪ/ → /hwʌɾ aɪ/（順行同化）

エリックの発話の中でも同化が起こっています。また、太字で示した talked や feel の母音部分にも注目しましょう。長母音が短く発音されるのは中国語英語の特徴のひとつです。

● When the professor **tal**ked about history,
　/wen ðə/ → /wen nə/（順行同化）

● She didn't have to feel sorry for me.
　　　/hæv tə/ → /hæf tə/（逆行同化）

Monologue

EC

■ *Ethnic perspectives in our future diverse society.*

1. Choose the phrase that is related to each word, and practice reading it out loud. 2-42

1. blend	( )	**(a)** a complete change in something
2. conservative	( )	**(b)** a sense of your own importance and value
3. dignity	( )	**(c)** a way of thinking about something
4. evolve	( )	**(d)** between people of different races
5. genuine	( )	**(e)** involving several different ethnicities of people
6. interracial	( )	**(f)** opposed to great or sudden social change
7. multi-ethnic	( )	**(g)** real; exactly what it appears to be
8. perspective	( )	**(h)** the act of giving up something valuable
9. sacrifice	( )	**(i)** to develop gradually
10. transformation	( )	**(j)** to form a mixture with something

2. Listen to the monologue and choose the best answer to each question. 2-43

1. Why did Mari talk about Tomoko?

   (A) Because Tomoko never thought about her ethnicity.

   (B) Because Tomoko will marry someone from another country.

   (C) Because Mari was born in China.

   (D) Because Mari wants to protect her own culture.

2. What is suggested about "conservative people"?

   (A) They don't know their own ethnicity.

   (B) They only speak one language.

   (C) They want to keep their own culture.

   (D) They embrace new cultures.

3. Look at the program.
   At what time did Mari give her presentation?

   (A) 9:30 – 11:00 AM.

   (B) 11:00 – 12:00 AM.

   (C) 1:00 – 2:30 PM.

   (D) 2:30 – 4:00 PM.

Schedule for Seminar on Cultural Diversity (* There are 3 seminarsforeach topic.)	
Time	**Topic**
8:30-9:30 AM	Registration and Breakfast
9:30-11:00 AM	Opening Talk (Prof. Jane Smith)
11:00 AM-12:00 PM	Diversity in the workplace
12:00-1:00 PM	Lunch
1:00-2:30 PM	Conserving our own cultures: What can the government do?
2:30-4:00 PM	Evolution of culture: Some viewpoints

3. Listen again and fill in the blanks with suitable forms of words in the previous page.

You are listening to Mari's presentation about her views on ethnic diversity. (repeat) 🎧 2-43

Good afternoon, and thank you for being here today. My name is Mari. Today, I would like to talk about how ethnic (1) _____ should change along with a diverse society.

First, I have a question for you. Have you ever thought about your ethnicity? I had never thought about it until my best friend Tomoko told me she is going to marry Kent, who is from China, next year. In our society, (2) _____ marriages are becoming more common. Therefore, there is no doubt that the number of (3) _____ children will be increasing in the future. Sooner or later, this trend will develop a brand-new culture that would fit into a diverse society.

However, some (4) _____ people, who want to protect their own cultures, make controversial statements about this trend. Some parents would like to pass on (5) _____ customs and traditions to the next generation. They seem to believe that human (6) _____ is rooted in ethnicity. If it is true, do people who have (7) _____ cultural backgrounds lose their dignity? I don't think that is true at all. Perhaps such people actually have the benefit of more than one cultural background.

In conclusion, human beings have experienced the (8) _____ of cultures since ancient times. Naturally, some cultures keep on (9) _____ whereas others might disappear. It is rare for a culture to remain unchanged. We should show respect when the vanishing cultures are (10) _____ and welcome new ones that are suitable for our new diverse society. Thank you for listening.

Speaking outline: *Inference (1)*

🎧 2-44

Suppose that you were born to parents with different ethnic backgrounds. What would be the good points? What would be the possible problems?

1) Premise	In modern society, there are children with multiple ethnic backgrounds. In this presentation, I will assume that I am in that position.
2) Inference 1	One of the good points about having multi-ethnic background would be _____ . I would take advantage of this by _____ .
3) Inference 2	On the other hand, I may run into difficulties when _____ . I would face the problem by _____ .
4) Conclusion	In conclusion, _____ .

Science and Scientists

科学について考えよう

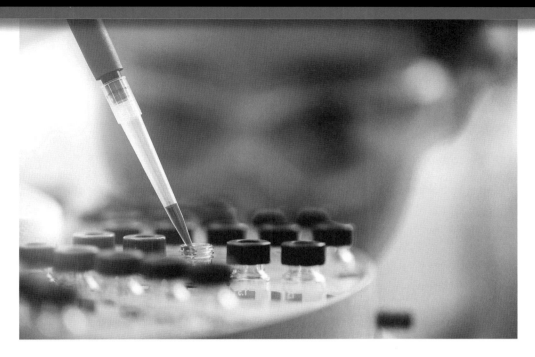

Warm-up: *Share your ideas.*

When you hear the word "science", what word comes to your mind first?

a. Computer science.

b. Humanities.

c. Natural science.

d. Science fiction.

> *I chose answer _____, because...*
> ....
> ....
> ....

Words in focus: *Search the internet for words and phrases.*

🎧 2-45

- ❏ co-presenter
- ❏ definition
- ❏ five senses
- ❏ human memorisation system
- ❏ learning style

- ❏ physical world
- ❏ retain information
- ❏ sci-fi movie
- ❏ scientific fact
- ❏ special effects

Dialogue

■ *What is science?*

1. Listen to each phrase, and guess what the speaker implies.　　　　　🔘 2-46

1. (　　)	(A) I'm pleased to be your partner.
2. (　　)	(B) I don't think they are based on facts.
3. (　　)	(C) Shall we explain the meanings of the word first?

2. Listen to the conversation and fill in the blanks.　　　　🔘 2-47, 48

Ken is talking with Sara, an exchange student from Egypt. They will give a presentation next week.

<Scene 1>

Sara: Ken, thank you for choosing me as your co-presenter for the next assignment. I'll do my best.

Ken: Thank *you* for joining me. (1) _____, but don't try too hard. Shall we get started?

Sara: Sure. The topic is "what is science," right? Do you have any ideas?

Ken: How about summarizing the history of sci-fi movies?

Sara: Ken? The professor wants us to talk about the meaning of "science," doesn't he?

Ken: Yes, something like that. The word "science" is included in science fiction movies, so it should be acceptable.

<Scene 2>

Sara: Well, do you think so? Science fiction.... Let's see.

Ken: This webpage says, "Science fiction films are movies which tell stories about the future, outer space, robots, or aliens."

Sara: And, "Science fiction movies often use special effects to show images of alien worlds or other planets far away."

Ken: Perfect! (2) _____

Sara: No, those are the definitions of sci-fi movies, not science. I don't think that sci-fi movies are suitable for this assignment. (3) _____ _____, either.

Ken: Okay, then, we'll define science first. And then explain how unscientific sci-fi movies are.

3. Listen to the conversation again and choose the best answer to each question. (repeat) 2-47, 48

\<Scene 1\>   What does Ken want to do?

(A) Give a presentation with Sara.

(B) Start talking about the topic.

(C) Summarize the history of sci-fi films.

(D) All of the above.

\<Scene 2\>   What was wrong with Ken's suggestion to research sci-fi movies?

(A) It doesn't tell stories about outer space.

(B) It would take too much time to cover.

(C) He misunderstood the main concept of the assignment.

(D) He copied another group's idea.

4. Listen to scenes 3 to 5, and choose the best answer to each question.   2-49, 50, 51

\<Scene 3\>   According to the Oxford Learner's Dictionary, what is science?

(A) Only scientists can practice science.

(B) It is based on facts that can be tested.

(C) It can be about imaginary planets.

(D) A sci-fi movie is a good example of a scientific fact.

\<Scene 4\>   Why is Ken confused?

(A) Because the dictionary shows something unreal.

(B) Because he is not good at literature.

(C) Because both science and fiction mean the same thing.

(D) Because the meaning of science and fiction are contradictory.

\<Scene 5\>   When will they need to have their presentation slides ready?

(A) By Tuesday.

(B) By Wednesday.

(C) By Thursday.

(D) By Friday.

ケンとサラが与えられた情報を元にして自分たちの発表準備を進める様子が表れているフレーズをもう一度聞き、書き取りましょう。

<Scene 1> 発表の主題	Sara: The _t_____ is "_w_____ is _s_____,_" right? Ken: How about _s_____ the _h_____ of _s_ – _m_____?
<Scene 2> Sci-fi 映画	Ken: Let's use those _d_____ for our _i_____ _p____. Sara: I _d___ _t____ that _s_ – _m_____ are _s_____ for this _a_____.
<Scene 3> 科学	Ken: _A_____ _w_____ and _f_ – _____ _p_____ are _n_____ _f_____. So, what is _s_____ _f_____? That's a _s_____ _c_____ of _w_____.
<Scene 4> フィクション	Ken: _F_____ _d_____ _s_____ _u_____. Sara: Yes, and we _c_____ _p_____ _f_____ about _p_____ and _e_____ that are _u_____.
<Scene 5> 発表準備	Sara: The _p_____ is going to be on _F_____ _m_____. Ken: Okay, we _s____ _h____ _f____ _m____ _d____. _L____ _s_____ with the _s_____ of the _s_____.

Pronunciation: *Intonation phrase* （音調単位） 🎵 2-52

会話の冒頭でサラとケンは二人とも "Thank you" と言っていますが、声の調子が異なります。ここでは、1つの文の区切りかた（音調単位）に注目してみましょう。音の強さ・高さ・長さは書き言葉には表れませんが、話者の意図や状態を示す有力な手がかりになります。

以下のサラの発話では、ひとつのフレーズの中で最後の内容語が最も強く高く長く発音されています。これが基本的な音調単位の中でのイントネーションです。

● **Ken, thank** you for **choos-** ing me.

一方、以下のケンの発話では you を強く高く長く発音し、直後に一瞬の空白を置いて「こちらこそ、ありがとう」という気持ちを表しています。

● **Thank** **you** / for **join-** ing me.

Monologue

EC

■ *How can you improve your learning?*

1. Choose the phrase that is related to each word, and practice reading it out loud. 🔴 2-53

1. duration	( )	**(a)** a systematic way of approaching something
2. efficiently	( )	**(b)** always and forever
3. method	( )	**(c)** in a way that does not last for long
4. permanently	( )	**(d)** in an organized, quick, and effective way
5. retain	( )	**(e)** not restricted in size, amount, or extent
6. sensory	( )	**(f)** something that sticks, like glue
7. sticky	( )	**(g)** the length of time
8. stimulate	( )	**(h)** to encourage something to become active
9. temporarily	( )	**(i)** to keep or continue to have something
10. unlimited	( )	**(j)** connected with the physical senses of touch, smell, taste, hearing, and sight

2. Listen to the monologue and choose the best answer to each question. 🔴 2-54

1. Which of the following stays in your brain for the shortest period?

   (A) Long-term memory.

   (B) Mid-term memory.

   (C) Sensory memory.

   (D) Short-term memory.

2. Look at the chart. Which of the following is the correct order of words to fill in the blanks?

   (A) ① Long-term, ② Sensory, and ③ Working.

   (B) ① Sensory, ② Working, and ③ Long-term.

   (C) ① Short-term, ② Long-term, and ③ Sensory.

   (D) ① Working, ② Long-term, and ③ Sensory.

3. What is true about the different types of memory?

   (A) Working memory lasts for several seconds.

   (B) Sensory memory involves only visual information.

   (C) Some parts of long-term memory can become short-term memory.

   (D) Some parts of short-term memory can become long-term memory.

Information
↓
①__ **Memory**
(several seconds)

Attention
↓
②__ **Memory**
(not permanent)

Repetition
↓
③__ **Memory**
(life-time)

3. Listen again and fill in the blanks with suitable forms of words in the previous page.

You are watching a broadcast on a science channel. (repeat) 🎧 2-54

What do you do when you need to memorise a ton of information? Do you know any strategies to (1) _____ increase your memory? (2) _____ memory, short-term memory, and long-term memory are three different types of memory. Each type has unique characteristics.

Sensory memory is the shortest type of memory. It is used when people have been (3) _____ by their five senses, which are sight, hearing, smell, taste, and touch. The (4) _____ of this memory is for several seconds. You can (5) _____ information in your brain (6) _____ with short-term memory, also known as working memory. This memory is like a (7) _____ note. You can have a look at the notes as much as you want, but they won't stay in your brain (8) _____. However, if you use the notes repeatedly, some of the memory will shift to long-term memory. Long-term memory consists of the survivors of short-term memory. The advantage of this memory is (9) _____ capacity. So, it can store the information, like how to type, for a life-time period.

The human memorisation system is unique, and it is a useful tool to improve your memory skills. Since each person has a different learning style, there is no particular training or activity that fits all. In other words, you are the one who needs to create your own (10) _____ that can enhance your learning experience. So, how can you use this knowledge about memory types to improve your learning?

Speaking outline: *Inference (2)* 🎧 2-55

Choose one theory that you think is interesting, and examine if it can be considered scientific.
e.g.) When you see someone yawning, you also yawn.

1) Premise	It is often said that _____. In this presentation, I will examine if this theory is scientific or not.
2) Inference 1	First, if it is scientific, it should be based on facts. An example of the facts that this theory is based on is _____. Thus / However, we can / cannot say that this theory is scientific.
3) Inference 2	Second, the scientific fact needs to be supported with evidence. According to _____, there is evidence / no evidence that _____.
4) Conclusion	In conclusion, I would say that _____.

Styles of Writing

書きことばと話しことばの違いについて考えよう

▋ **Warm-up:** *Share your ideas.*

What do you pay the most attention to when writing in English?

   a. Avoiding grammar errors.

   b. Making sentences short.

   c. Including catchy phrases.

   d. Reaching the minimum word count.

I chose answer _____, because…
....
....
....

▋ **Words in focus:** *Search the internet for words and phrases.* 🎧 2-56

❏ colloquialism

❏ English essay

❏ filler words

❏ front page

❏ news article

❏ newspaper headline

❏ tense

❏ word count

❏ wording

❏ written and spoken language

Dialogue

■ *The strange world of newspaper headlines.*

1. Listen to each phrase, and guess what the speaker implies. 🎧 2-57

1. (   )   (A) a special rule that people keep
2. (   )   (B) I haven't reached my goal yet.
3. (   )   (C) what the readers expect in newspapers

2. Listen to the conversation and fill in the blanks. 🎧 2-58, 59

Mari is talking with Julius, a journalist from Rwanda.

<Scene 1>

Mari: Julius, congratulations! Your news article made the front page!

Julius: Thanks, Mari. But (1) _____ Anything you noticed?

Mari: Actually, the wording looks a bit strange to me.

Julius: Which part? With newspapers, there's (2) _____
_____ .

Mari: The headline says "Japanese Comedian *Visits* Rwanda." But it happened last week. Shouldn't it be the past tense *Visited*?

Julius: I see. With newspaper headlines, we use the present tense to explain past events.

<Scene 2>

Mari: But how come you use the present tense?

Julius: It's pretty simple if you think about (3) _____
_____ .

Mari: We read it for, um, to get the latest information.

Julius: Exactly. The word *visits* sounds a lot more recent than *visited*.

Mari: In other words, it sounds more interesting to readers?

Julius: Yep. Is there anything else that you found?

3. Listen to the conversation again and choose the best answer to each question. (repeat)  2-58, 59

<Scene 1> Why did Mari congratulate Julius?

        (A) He received a prize for good journalism.

        (B) He improved his English considerably.

        (C) He published in the most important part of the newspaper.

        (D) He finished his studies in Rwanda.

<Scene 2> According to Mari, what do people read newspapers for?

        (A) To learn new vocabulary.

        (B) To understand difficult concepts.

        (C) To gather up-to-date information.

        (D) To enjoy local gossip.

4. Listen to scenes 3 to 5, and choose the best answer to each question. 2-60, 61, 62

<Scene 3> What is one rule about headlines?

        (A) To make them as wordy as possible.

        (B) To make them as brief as possible.

        (C) To write them using an interesting font.

        (D) To write them using different colors.

<Scene 4> What does Mari imply about her writing assignments?

        (A) They need to be done within a set time limit.

        (B) They need to be edited by a professional writer.

        (C) They require a minimum of 500 words.

        (D) They require a maximum of 500 words.

<Scene 5> What is true about Mari and Julius when they write?

        (A) Mari writes fast, but takes her time to edit.

        (B) Julius writes fast, but takes his time to edit.

        (C) Both Mari and Julius write slowly.

        (D) Both Mari and Julius edit slowly.

ジュリアスと話すことによってマリの疑問が解消されていく様子が表れているフレーズをもう一度聞き、書き取りましょう。

<Scene 1> 現在形	**Mari:**	The h_____ says, "J_____ C_____ _Visits_ R_____."
	Julius:	With newspaper headlines, we use the p_____ t_____ to e_____ p_____ e_____.
<Scene 2> 現在形を使う 理由	**Mari:**	But how come you u____ the p_____ t_____?
	Julius:	The word V_____ sounds a lot more r_____ than V_____.
<Scene 3> スペースの節約	**Mari:**	There is a_____ h_____. "D____ S_____ to H_____ R_____"
	Julius:	Yes, at least it's a f_____ l_____ s_____ than s_____ _____ or is g_____ to.
<Scene 4> 語数制限	**Mari:**	I s_____ h_____ t_____ to i_____ my w_____ c_____ to _____ _____.
	Julius:	I w____ I c____ g__ s_____ for 500 m_____ w_____.
<Scene 5> 修正のための 時間	**Mari:**	You e_____ your w_____ to m_____ it s_____?
	Julius:	Yes. I've h_____ that the g_____ w_____ s_____ the m_____ time on e_____ their w_____.

マリとジュリアスはカジュアルな場面で会話しているため、言いよどみがあったり、口語調の発音を用いたりしています。以下の発言は、改まった場面ではどう発音されるか、考えてみましょう。

<Scene 2> Mari: But how come you use the present tense?

→ But w____ d____ you use the present tense?

<Scene 3> Mari: You mean, you wanna save some space in the headline?

→ You mean, you w_____ t____ save some space in the headline?

<Scene 3> Mari: I've gotta write a lot more to try and reach that level!

→ I h_____ t____ write a lot more to try and reach that level!

Monologue

EC

■ *Your presentation should be different from your essay.*

1. Choose the phrase that is related to each word, and practice reading it out loud. CD 2-64

1. aloud	( )	**(a)** a part of a play or film
2. casual	( )	**(b)** a word or short phrase used when you pause to think
3. colloquialism	( )	**(c)** an informal word or expression
4. complicated	( )	**(d)** being almost, but not exactly, the same
5. revise	( )	**(e)** in a voice loud enough to be heard
6. filler	( )	**(f)** difficult to understand
7. real-time	( )	**(g)** not formal
8. scene	( )	**(h)** not needed or wanted
9. similar	( )	**(i)** to change or correct a piece of writing
10. unnecessary	( )	**(j)** at the same time as events actually happen

2. Listen to the monologue and choose the best answer to each question. CD 2-65

1. What is the main purpose of the talk?

(A) To discuss different dialects.

(B) To compare English in different contexts.

(C) To review a favorite movie.

(D) To teach students about PowerPoint.

2. Look at slides A, B, and C. Which did Mari use?

(A) Slide A.

(B) Slide B.

(C) Slide C.

(D) None of the above.

3. What does Mari mean when she says, "spoken English is in real-time"?

(A) You cannot cancel what you talked about.

(B) Only real people can speak well.

(C) It refers to things that exist in our world.

(D) People cannot speak for a long time.

Slide A

This movie has exciting action scenes.... like, uh, the final action scene when the villain finally dies.

Slide B

This movie has exciting action scenes such as the final action scene when the villain finally dies.

Slide C

This movie has exciting action scenes (e.g., the final action scene when the villain finally dies).

3. Listen again and fill in the blanks with suitable forms of words in the previous page.

(repeat) 2-65

You are listening to Mari's presentation on differences between written and spoken language.

Today I will present on the topic, "What's Written and Spoken English?". We often see different forms of English used in different situations. For example, your essay could sound quite different from a presentation. Therefore, I'd like to talk about the differences between spoken and written English.

First, spoken English tends to have (1) _____ and (2) _____ words. Colloquialisms are casual words like "wanna," that can be a short form of English words. Filler words are sounds you put in your speech when you're trying to think of what to say. For example, I say "um," a lot. Do you have something (3) _____ in your first language?

Next, with written English, we make sentences more (4) _____ than spoken English, and try to be clear about what we mean. Please look at the sentence on this slide. How would you read these two letters aloud, right after the word "(5) _____" on the second line? Well, many of you just read the thing (6) _____, saying "E-G." Actually, it's better to say "For example" in place of "e.g."

So, why do these differences happen? One reason is because spoken English is in (7) _____. By this, I mean that once we speak, we can't take it back. We want to speak so it's easy for the listener to understand. That's why spoken sentences can sound (8) _____ and short. Written English, however, is not in real-time. Writers can (9) _____ their work and delete (10) _____ words. In the next slide, I'll show you what I mean.

Speaking outline: *Paraphrasing*

 2-66

Find a news article written in English, and paraphrase it into spoken English.

1) Introduction	Hi, I'm _____. Have you ever heard of the news about _____? I found it on _____.
2) Paraphrasing	It happened in [explain WHO did WHAT, WHERE, WHEN, HOW/WHY].
3) Your opinion	I think [explain what you think/feel about this news].

Appendix

　本書の dialogue (アメリカ英語では dialog と綴ることもあります) では、日本の大学生が世界の様々な地域の出身者と会話をする場面を紹介したため、聞き慣れない発音が含まれていたかもしれません。同様に、使われる英語表現・語彙・綴りにも、可能な限り地域性を反映させました。本書では英語表現・語彙・綴りを大まかにアメリカ式・イギリス式に分け、以下の基準で表記しました。なお、パンクチュエーションに関しては、アメリカ式に統一しました。

・アメリカ式
キャプションや指示文・質問・解答選択肢・日本、アメリカ、ブラジル出身者の発話。
・イギリス式
イギリス、アイルランド、ニュージーランド、シンガポール、インド、ロシア、中国、エジプト、ルワンダ出身者の発話。

　以下は、英米の地域差が表れやすい英語表現・語彙・綴りの例です。(カッコ内の数字) は、該当の表現や語が扱われているユニットです。

・表現や文法
過去形と現在完了形の使い分けや、前置詞の使い方、動詞の過去形の末尾などが異なることがあります。
例) (U2) US You already started.... ― UK You've already started....
　　(U4) US on weekends ― UK at weekends
　　(U6, 12) US different from/than ― UK different to/from
　　(U7) US she has learned ― UK she has learnt
　　(U1, 6, 11) US take a look/break ― UK have a look/break

・語彙
同じものを指しているのに単語が異なるケースや、同じ単語が別のものを指すケースがあります。
例) (U1, 4, 8) US college ― UK university　　(U4) US mom ― UK mum
　　(U1) US semester ― UK term　　　　　　(U7) US résumé ― UK CV
　　(U3) US bathroom ― UK toilet　　　　　(U11) US movie ― UK film
　　(U3) US flashlight ― UK torch　　　　　(U12) US um ― UK erm
　　(U3) US elevator ― UK lift

・綴り
以下の例の他にも、語末が -ize と -ise、-or と -our、-er と -re のように異なる単語は多くあります。
例) (U1) US industrialize ― UK industrialise　　(U7) US color ― UK colour
　　(U1) US organize ― UK organise　　　　　(U9) US defense ― UK defence
　　(U2, 3, 6) US program ― UK programme　(U11) US memorization ―
　　(U3) US rumor ― UK rumour　　　　　　　　　 UK memorisation
　　(U5) US honor ― UK honour

TEXT PRODUCTION STAFF

edited by	編集
Hiroko Nakazawa	中澤 ひろ子

English-language editing by	英文校正
Bill Benfield	ビル・ベンフィールド

cover design by	表紙デザイン
Nobuyoshi Fujino	藤野 伸芳

text design by	本文デザイン
Nobuyoshi Fujino	藤野 伸芳

CD PRODUCTION STAFF

narrated by	吹き込み者
Chris Koprowski (American English)	クリス・コプロスキ（アメリカ英語）
Jennifer Okano (American English)	ジェニファー・オカノ（アメリカ英語）
Emma Howard (British English)	エマ・ハワード（イギリス英語）
Sarah Greaves (Australian English)	サラ・グリーブズ（オーストラリア英語）
et al.	他

Global Perspectives
Listening & Speaking Book 2

2023年1月20日　初版発行
2024年3月 5 日　第3刷発行

編著者　中西 のりこ　Nicholas Musty　大竹 翔子

　　　　Tam Shuet Ying　海老原 由貴　藤村 敬次

発行者　佐野 英一郎

発行所　株式会社 成 美 堂
　　　　〒101-0052 東京都千代田区神田小川町 3-22
　　　　TEL 03-3291-2261　　FAX 03-3293-5490
　　　　http://www.seibido.co.jp

印刷・製本　（株）倉敷印刷

ISBN 978-4-7919-7262-3　　　　　　　　　　　　Printed in Japan